When
Critical
Thinking
met **English**
Literature

More related titles

Critical Thinking for AS Level
Roy van den Brink-Budgen

Critical Thinking for A2
Roy van den Brink-Budgen

Critical Thinking for Students
Learn the skills of critical assessment and effective argument

'A really useful introduction to developing and improving a core skill.'
– Association of Commonwealth Universities Bulletin

Writing an Essay
Simple techniques to transform your coursework and examinations

'There is a lot of good sense in this book.' – Times Educational Supplement

howto**books**

Please send for a free copy of the latest catalogue:
How To Books
Spring Hill House, Spring Hill Road
Begbroke, Oxford OX5 1RX, United Kingdom
info@howtobooks.co.uk

www.howtobooks.co.uk

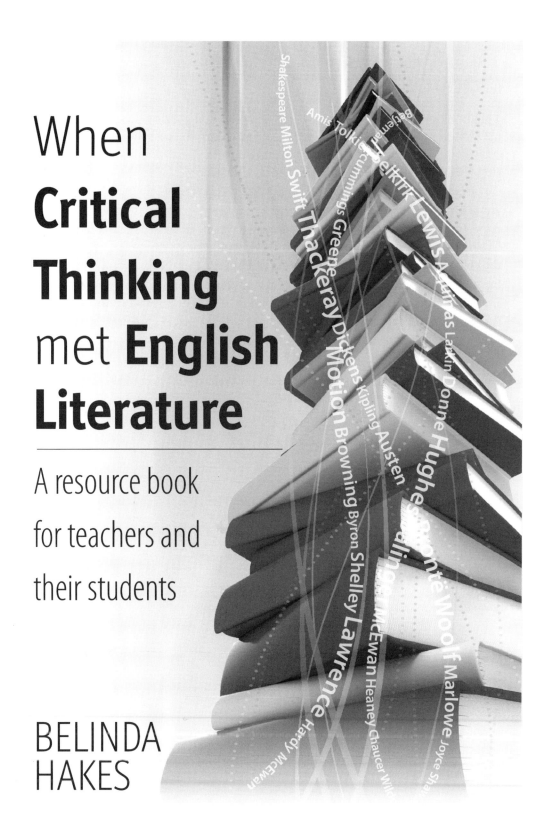

When **Critical Thinking** met **English Literature**

A resource book
for teachers and
their students

BELINDA
HAKES

howto books

DEDICATION

This book is for Terry, who gives me the precious gifts of time and space, and for all our family for their interest and encouragement.

ACKNOWLEDGEMENTS

My thanks first go to Roy van den Brink-Budgen, second only to Socrates in the critical thinking world, and without whom this book would never have been started. Thanks also to my friend, colleague and partner-in-crime Noel Stewart, without whose infectious enthusiasm it probably wouldn't have been finished. Thanks to Nikki and Giles, for taking the risk, to my editor, Nick Hutchins, and to the students of Wyke Sixth Form College, for inspiring me and going along with my weird ideas. Live long, read much and think well!

How To Books Ltd
Spring Hill House, Spring Hill Road
Begbroke, Oxford OX5 1RX, United Kingdom
Tel: 01865 375794 Fax: 01865 379162
info@howtobooks.co.uk
www.howtobooks.co.uk

British Library Cataloguing in Publication Data
A catalogue record for this book is available from
the British Library.

First published 2008

ISBN: 978 1 84528 317 9

Cover design by Baseline Arts Ltd, Oxford
Produced for How To Books by Deer Park Productions, Tavistock
Typeset by *specialist* publishing services ltd, Montgomery
Printed and bound by Cromwell Press Ltd, Trowbridge, Wiltshire

Contents

Introduction

Critical thinking is often seen as a new subject. But, of course, though the name might be new, the subject isn't. Those of us engaged in it are, at best, dwarfs standing on the shoulders of giants. In this position, of course, dwarfs are supposed to be able to see further than the giants. Sometimes, however, people in critical thinking seem to be looking down rather than towards the horizon. They need to have their heads lifted. Here is a book that should help this to happen.

For me, one of the greatest thinkers of all time was Peter Abelard. But, if he's known at all these days, it's normally only for his love of Heloïse and the price he paid for that relationship. However, in his time, many saw him as the greatest philosopher since Aristotle. He was a brilliant logician, an outstanding teacher of logic, and was pre-eminent in rhetoric. And this tells us something. We have come to see the world (though we stand on others' shoulders) in ways that impoverish our thinking. We see the study of literature as having little or even nothing to tell us about the study of critical thinking (and vice versa). However, for Abelard (seeing very clearly by standing on the shoulders of Aristotle), an understanding of language lay at the root of all intellectual endeavour. He had learned that the composition of prose and verse (rhetoric) was a necessary step to a deeper understanding of logic. Indeed a contemporary epitaph describes him as being the bridge of rhetoric to the mountain of logic. It always strikes me as odd that, in today's attempts at the assessment of critical thinking, the term 'rhetoric' is used by many of those who write the papers as an example of poor argumentation. The student who uses 'mere rhetoric' is castigated for not being a good Critical Thinker.

So how have we come to this? How have we divorced an appreciation of prose and verse from critical thinking? This could be the subject of another book but, in the meantime, let us be pleased that we have someone who has made a contribution to rebuilding the bridge of rhetoric to the mountain of logic. Some of you might remember that, for some time, I have been speaking rather darkly of 'a lady in Hull' who has been doing important work in linking the teaching of literature and critical thinking. Well, here is that lady.

I have been involved in critical thinking for 21 years and have read a great deal of material on the subject. Unfortunately, much of the stuff that's written on it these days is remarkable for its lack of passion, its lack of intellectual excitement, its lack of fun. Using my own criteria of judgement, much of the stuff that's written on critical thinking fails to make itself on to my bookshelves, being relegated instead to a filing cabinet drawer. This book, however, will sit proudly on one of my shelves, sharing space with the likes of Abelard, Darwin, and Voltaire (as well as Donne and Keats).

This book has made me think differently and, for that, I'm very grateful. This book should make all of us look at literature differently. It should certainly make us look at critical thinking differently. There's nothing here of the passionless, of the unexciting, of the humourless recitals of tedious and artificial argument. Take for example, Belinda's examination of Donne's poem 'The Flea'. Her showing this to be a remarkable chat-up approach through analogy is one that students will want to take apart, will want to evaluate (and, perhaps, will want to use). This is so much better than so many of the heart-deadening analogies that critical thinking students are given. For another example, take her examination of 'The Ancient Mariner'. Here students can look at issues of causation and correlation in a new way. What is the significance of the shooting of the albatross? *Post hoc* becomes central to the anguish, to notions of right and wrong.

So who is this book for? It's obviously for English teachers. They will find that, at one level, there is much here that might be familiar (and Belinda writes in a way that acknowledges their knowledge and expertise). But they will see the familiar in unfamiliar ways. They will find reasoning in poems; they will be intrigued by the finding of assumptions in narrative; they will find troublesome issues of credibility in all sorts of first-person accounts. For those English teachers who also teach critical thinking, this is a book that will transform their teaching, showing the richness of the connections they can make between the two subjects.

But the book should also have a much wider readership. For those of us whose academic background is not English, there might seem to be dangers in tackling some of the material that's in here. But critical thinking invites us to take risks. What does this mean? What is the significance of that? How could we explain this? What inference can be drawn from that? We're used to taking such risks with our material, such that a student might well come up with something we hadn't thought of before. So, if you teach critical thinking, but don't have a background in English, use this book to show you how to risk looking at literature in your teaching. Use it to add to your skills. Use it to encourage more cross-curricular links, teaching, and programmes.

As Abelard explained, "spiritual men have made better progress in sacred doctrine by the study of literature than by the merits of religion". I'm sure that he would want to update that pronouncement by saying "Critical Thinkers will make better progress in their thinking by studying literature than by just looking at what's published in the majority of critical thinking books." And I'm sure that, having read this book, you'll agree.

Roy van den Brink-Budgen

Preface
Critical Thinking and English Literature

This is the story of a journey, a journey between what appeared to be two islands but which, it transpires, are simply different coastlines of the same one.

Once upon a time I lived in Literature Land, responding on an emotional, indeed visceral level, to the magic of the literary canon of FR Leavis. Magic, please note, does not appear in any glossary I have relating to A level critical thinking: what could it and English literature possibly have in common?

At university I discovered linguistics, but despite my degree comprising an equal amount of it and "literature" neither I nor my lecturers made any connection between the two. Indeed, my subsidiary philosophy course created more of an interface, as the texts we studied were invariably written in language every bit as seductive as the ideas which they expressed.

It wasn't until the mid 80s that, having taught English literature for some years, I discovered A level English language and realised the blindingly obvious: literature comprises language. Yes, it is written by people, yes it is read by people, and those people eat, sleep, and have their own lives set against their own contexts: even linguistic analysis allows for pragmatic aspects to be borne in mind. But the notion that one could take a line of poetry and explore its intricacy, precision and exquisiteness through linguistic analysis came to me with great excitement, both in terms of the intrinsic pleasure of the exercise – here, at last, was something objectively verifiable in literature – but also in what it revealed of the writer's methods. This changed the way I taught. It didn't replace my previous approach, but enhanced it: not only could we talk about *what* the text meant, but *how* it meant. My personal epiphany occurred when I was reading Philip Larkin's poem 'Here', from *The Whitsun Weddings* collection. The first stanza, of nine lines, begins with a present participle, "Swerving", which is repeated three times before we get to the finite verb "Gathers" which is the first word of the second stanza. Straightforward grammatical analysis reveals just how Larkin achieved so much movement in these ten lines, mimetic of the way in which the north-south axis of England has to be diverged from when a traveller is aiming for Hull and the plain of Holderness. Swerving *describes* movement, yes, but present participles are, by definition, non-finite: the swerving just keeps going – until that finite verb "Gathers", in "Gathers to the surprise of a large town". Gathers? What gathers? What's the subject of this finite verb? Why, swerving, of course. A present participle as the subject of a sentence: no wonder there's so much sense of movement! I have subsequently read any number of observations of this grammatical source of movement in the poem, enhancing the lexical and semantic choices Larkin made, but the pleasure I felt in discovering it for myself cannot be diminished.

That little analytical edge, the precise analytical tool of grammar, gave me more to offer my students; gave them another colour on their palette. This, however, is a long way from the logical, almost mathematical world of critical thinking A level: I may have realised that Literature Land and Linguistics Land were parts of the same island, but critical thinking was still a long way off, both geographically, temporally and temperamentally.

Some years ago I became responsible in my college for curriculum development (latterly "Learning and Staff Development") and one of my remits was to consider both new things to teach and new ways of teaching. This was how the then new critical thinking AS came to my attention; as Head of English it is unlikely that I would have thought that this was anything I could personally engage with, let alone teach.

I invited the college's Head of Philosophy to consider having a go with a small pilot group (an unintentional but apt extension of the travelling metaphor). I had gone through specimen questions but found myself repeatedly trying to get out of the self-contained reasoning structures. I also kept getting the wrong answers, and even fell back into the comfort zone where "I can't do this" is a statement of permanent fact rather than a starting point for learning.

The success of the pilot group led to critical thinking AS being established in the curriculum and I thought that that was that, until the Advanced Extension Awards cruise ship hove into view and invited me on board, with its colourful flags, its swimming pool, techno gym and well stocked bar.

Whatever the future of Advanced Extension Awards, in terms of the possibility of A* A levels, I do hope that AEA critical thinking remains. It is unique as an AEA in drawing from students across any subject, and as such can and should draw staff from any subject. This new examination seemed to offer a wonderful opportunity for teaching across curricular barriers, for opening a door to peer learning amongst teachers and exploring new and exciting ways of teaching and learning.

At A level what we do is not only subject specific, but even unit specific: my own students of literature, in an uncanny echo of my university experience, seem surprised if asked to consider connections between different units of their A level, never mind with other subjects. And as teachers, here we are in a learning community, but what are we learning from each other? How can teachers be encouraged to explore peer learning and to encourage students to make useful connections within and across their subjects? Pondering these questions I felt it was time I put into practice what I was trying to encourage in others, and began collaboration on AEA with my colleague in philosophy. While he took sessions on logic, I brought the AEA English students (a few of whom had chosen AEA critical thinking anyway) onto the ship.

The thing about a cruise ship is that on the one hand it's familiar and safe, but on the other hand it can take us exploring and adventuring and discovering. (Not that I've ever been on a cruise, but then Shakespeare never went to Italy.) (Or did he? Or did he, but was he Christopher Marlowe?) (These are relevant asides!)

We each brought our own experience, expertise and approach to the AEA sessions, which comprised three-hour extravaganzas, either off-site, on Saturdays or in the holidays. We challenged students; they worked collaboratively, thought laterally, creatively and logically by turns; students of maths worked with students of art or English, chemistry with history.

We devised a session on *Meaning and Metaphor*, which covered the dangers (and fun) inherent in equivocation, the need for precision in deductive reasoning and at the same time showed how metaphor can reach a truth beyond the literal. Another time we looked at the film *Memento* and explored making meaning through narrative structures and point-of-view. We also did a session entitled *Logical Literature?*

Of course, while the students were learning from my colleague, so was I, and I put my toe into the pedagogic pool on the ship, wondering what might happen if I looked at some examples of persuasive and argumentative texts in literature, and tried to apply some techniques and approaches from critical thinking.

The next time I taught *Othello* I found myself treating Iago not just as an intriguing, brilliant and possibly insane character, but as an expert in fallacious argument, the components of which I could identify with precise terminology, for my students' admiration (of Iago and Shakespeare, not me!). We marked up Act II scene (i) ll 216 – 243, the scene where Iago convinces Roderigo that Cassio is his enemy. We found the conclusion, that is the thing which the author – Iago – wants the reader or listener to accept as true. We found intermediate conclusions which supported that conclusion; we found evidence and we found analogy. Roderigo just couldn't cope with this. Othello was harder work for Iago, but in III (iii) we find Othello moving from saying of Desdemona "… I do love thee; and when I love thee not, / Chaos is come again" to arranging for her to be spied upon, and asking himself, "Why did I marry?" Iago achieves this at first by what he *doesn't* say – he appears reticent, and Othello's inference is that he is withholding hurtful or damaging information. Othello repeatedly has to urge him to speak more and by the time he does he is saying, "I speak not yet of proof" (a sure way of suggesting that there is some), and bases his eventual accusation of Desdemona's on a false analogy, over generalising from all Venetian women to Desdemona – perhaps in an echo of Brabantio's stinging words to Othello to the effect that since Desdemona had deceived her father she would probably deceive Othello.

Perhaps if Othello had studied critical thinking and applied credibility criteria he might not have been set on a course of self-destruction. Certainly, Hamlet could have benefited a great deal from it, when trying to judge whether to believe his father's ghost or whether to accept that Claudius came by the throne and queen honestly. Hamlet is, however, willing to work along critical thinking lines sometimes, as we see in "To be or not to be" – another very rewarding passage when analysed according to critical thinking approach.

Bringing critical thinking to Shakespeare has proved a worthwhile additional way of exploring the texts. As well as the two mentioned above, *Coriolanus, Measure for Measure*, *The Merchant of Venice* and *Much Ado About Nothing* have so far worked well. Indeed, any play, or any novel which includes dialogue and debate, can be viewed through the eyes of a critical thinker. Look at Stoppard, Becket, and Wilde, and although it's not yet made it to the syllabus, try the opening scene of *Reservoir Dogs* for a cracking example of argument in scripted dialogue.

The same texts can be used with both English and critical thinking classes. John Donne famously uses metaphors from mathematics, science, astronomy and cartography in his love poems and often favours giving the poems argument structures and lexis:

Marke but this flea, and marke in this,
How little that which thou deny'st me is…

The opening words of 'The Flea' tell us straight away that we're in some sort of reasoned argument, in this case based on analogy. What students can try is to apply criteria for judging the strength of this analogy. These criteria will have been learnt and frequently applied in critical thinking, but are a valuable discussion focus for the English students. *The flea has bitten me and absorbed a drop of my blood; it then did the same with you. Our blood is already, thereby, mingled – is this anything for you to be ashamed of?* The bells of equivocation are already ringing. (Interestingly, my students like equivocations and fallacies best of all – perhaps because it's so good to spot them in other people's arguments – surely not because they're so good to use in their own!) Both literature and critical thinking students found it a challenge, but the text retained its integrity and indeed Donne's skill and bravado were enhanced in the eyes of all.

My critical thinking students have not only analysed poetry; they used the great Marlowe/Shakespeare debate as an exercise in investigating the credibility of evidence, looking at documents ranging from the report on Marlowe's inquest to analyses emanating from Shakespeare and Marlowe scholars alike. Oh, and they learnt a bit about literature too.

Somewhere on this journey, from English literature to English language to AEA critical thinking I made the latest discovery, which was that I could have a real go at actually teaching A level critical thinking. I awaited my first results with the trepidation and excitement of a novice, hoping that I had done well for my students and enabled them to do well for themselves. I have found the work challenging and stimulating. I have introduced literary texts to critical thinking, and critical thinking approaches in English literature, and am continually learning from this practice. The benefit has gone beyond A level, to GCSE re-sit classes, where students need to be able to construct arguments and to be analytical and inferential readers of non-fiction texts.

My journey of discovery continues; this book provides holiday snaps of some of the highlights so far.

1
Othello

…when I love thee not,
Chaos is come again.

Why did I marry? This honest creature doubtless
Sees and knows more, much more, than he unfolds.

The first quotation is an indication of the power of Othello's feelings for Desdemona; the second is as a result of the words, only the words, of the calumnious Iago: what has happened in between?

I teach critical thinking in the hope that it will enable students to have more control over their worlds rather than less; that they will question, will not be manipulated, and will demand answers. If only Othello had been in one of my classes.

In between the two extracts above, no facts have changed. Othello's wife, Desdemona, has not been unfaithful. He is right to say that when he stops loving her, chaos will come.

As I have mentioned in my introductory chapter, I didn't find the idea of critical thinking amenable, any more, perhaps, than readers of this book might if they are from an English teaching background. Whenever I looked at the extracts in the exam papers I wanted to say, yes, but … to add contextual features and individual readings. I found the logic quite difficult: not to understand, but to warm to. However, appreciation and astonishment can creep up on us unawares, like love.

Only a little while after being peripherally involved with critical thinking I was looking at *Othello* with an A2 literature group, and wondering why, how, Iago manages to do what he does. As a way in, I looked at how he convinces Roderigo (admittedly, not too much of a challenge) of the possibility that Desdemona may be interested in him. Yes, it's clear that Roderigo will hear what he wants to hear, but there's surely more to it than that. And the "more" hadn't occurred to me until after I'd learnt a little about critical thinking and shrugged off some of my prejudice.

On the whiteboard I wrote down the key statements of Iago's argument:

- Desdemona loved very passionately and fell in love very quickly (true).
- She loved Othello's stories (true).

At this point, we can see Roderigo being lulled into accepting the argument, simply because it begins with indisputably true premises.

- This is temporary. (We can't accept this: it's simply an unsubstantiated claim. Iago needs to justify this for us. However, he has no need to bother justifying it to Roderigo, who is hearing just what he hoped to hear.)
- She needs to like what she sees. (Again, this can't be disputed.)
- Once the stories stop, she'll really see Othello. (He's implying that the stories will stop and that they were somehow masking the "real" Othello, which she won't like. All these things can be disputed.)
- Othello is ugly. (To Iago? But that's hardly relevant to Desdemona; however, Roderigo must be loving this.)
- Therefore she can't keep loving him.

So far: we have two true statements, but then the claim that this is temporary. Why is it? Well, the implication is that he will eventually have no more stories. We have the argument that Desdemona's aesthetic sense must be satisfied, and the claim that, once the charm of the stories has worn off, Desdemona will realise that Othello is not pleasing to the eye, and so there will be nothing to keep her loving him.

Even the sex will become dull, through familiarity (does this say more about Iago than Desdemona?).

2

So, no more stories; dull sex; ugly man: she'll then realise that they have nothing in common. Then she'll find him repellent. Therefore she'll look for someone else.

"This granted" – i.e., assuming this to be true (a massive assumption, which Roderigo is powerless to challenge) then who will it be? (Of course Roderigo hopes it's him, but Iago can't miss the opportunity to attack Cassio.)

- It must be Cassio (conclusion).
- Why (reasons): he talks well (and that was one of things that she fell for about Othello).
- Being a good talker, he'll be able to be duplicitous (well, he may have the capability, but that doesn't mean he'd ever use it).
- He is good looking and young.

Roderigo has no chance; this is too easy for Iago, but a nice warm up for his uncompromising destruction of Othello's faith in Desdemona in Act III scene (iii).

I feel almost embarrassed about my excitement upon reading this as a fallacious argument: why hadn't I seen it before in this way? Previously I worked though it with students as a very persuasive speech, but never with the same sense of this being the beginning of something really special: I could bring my learning from critical thinking into my teaching of literature. I ran off to get my colleague who teaches critical thinking, fervently hoping that my "please don't wipe this off" message would be prominent enough for our meticulous cleaner.

I couldn't wait to get back to the play, and to interrogate the scene in which Iago faultlessly turns Othello's assured love into bitter regret. How did he do this?

This part of the play is an excellent one for sub-texting: underwriting the lines of the characters with the moves made in the argument. In terms of a game of chess, Iago is the one who understands the rules. Othello, like Roderigo, is guileless, and thus an easy target.

So, here's a look at the moves which Iago makes in III (iii) 11 90 – 254; lines the effect of which turn the story of Othello and Desdemona from romance to tragedy, and result in her murder, his suicide and – what, for Iago? We'll never know.

At the start of this scene, Othello openly expresses his love for Desdemona; however, Iago responds with what appears to be a moment of reticence: "My noble lord ...". This implies that he has something to say, yet does not wish to say it. The start of the strategy though which he is to turn the burden of proof onto Othello: Iago need not (of course, cannot) prove Desdemona's guilt, therefore, Othello must prove, to his own satisfaction, her innocence. This is the corruption of reasoning that manifests itself in Miller's *The Crucible*, where false accusations are made out of nothing, yet the burden of proof lies not with the accuser but with the victim. Only maybe this is worse; for although Othello is a victim, of Iago's wickedness, it is Desdemona who pays the price.

Elsewhere in this book we look at credibility of evidence, and this can be a very interesting way into the study of this scene. However, at the moment we're more interested in the ploys which Iago uses to move Othello from security to insecurity, from bliss to misery, from harmony to discord.

Is that unfinished "My noble lord ..." an appeal to ignorance? Inviting Othello to imagine that something must be the case because he doesn't know that it isn't?

It seems that Iago may well be working along these lines; his next words link Desdemona and Cassio, reminding Othello of their earlier intimacy. Why, Othello asks, do you want to know this? "But for a satisfaction of my thought; No further harm." Again, implying something withheld.
The bait is interesting to Othello: "Why of thy thought?" Othello explains that Cassio was a frequent traveller between the two lovers; Iago's one word response "Indeed?" undermines the innocence of Othello's memory. Is there now a tiny doubt: "Is he not honest?" "Honest, my lord?" Again, appearing to withhold something; being reluctant to disclose something, thus suggesting that there is something to be disclosed. Honest – "for aught I know": this makes the judgement subjective and fallible (contrast this with II (ii) 216 ff, where he blatantly makes subjective judgements appear objective) "What

dost thou think?" Othello wants to know. Again, the delaying tactic of simply repeating the question, implying reluctance to answer. Othello is now falling, inexorably into the trap:

> *Think, my lord? Alas, thou echoest me,*
> *As if there were some monster in thy thought*
> *Too hideous to be shown. Thou dost mean something.*

Suddenly, Othello begins re-interpreting the previous words and events, writing Iago's script for him.

And then, "If thou dost love me / Show me thy thought." This highlights a major flaw in Othello: belief in the teller is misplaced, but combined with Othello's insecurity it is strong enough to overcome the incredibility of the idea. That said, if Othello were to apply credibility criteria to Iago he might be no better than we, as at the heart is a gaping hole where Iago's motive may lie. This is Shakespeare's genius: we never know. And so we endlessly debate.

After "Show me thy thought" Iago prevaricates again, increasing Othello's apprehension. Othello acknowledges that Iago "weigh'st [his] words before [he] giv'st them breath" but only we know that the motive for this is not compassion. Iago's hesitancy is alarming Othello: "these stops of thine affright me": exactly as intended ...

Iago's next move involves a cunning use of grammar and syntax: "For Michael Cassio, I dare be sworn I think that he is honest." Implication: maybe he isn't. Reinforced by "Men should be what they seem": which appears to be a principle to agree with, but which in this context implies that Cassio is otherwise.

Othello's "Nay, yet there's more in this." shows us that Othello now believes that there really is something being withheld. This apparent withholding continues and continues, until Othello is almost pleading to be told. Iago is self-deprecating in "I do beseech you ... my thoughts", but this only adds to his credibility in Othello's eyes. He goes on to talk about "woman", still apparently reluctant to speak directly of Desdemona. So ensnared is Othello now that he exclaims "By heaven, I'll know thy thoughts." This is what Iago has achieved, with no evidence and, in truth, no claims. His case is another black hole which sucks all Othello's confidence while having no substance of its own.

The game continues, with Iago refusing to disclose his thoughts (so, it must be *really* serious) and then warning Othello to beware of jealousy. This may be good advice, but it is logically unconnected with anything else. Of course it is connected by association, contiguity, juxtaposition – whichever predominates in Othello's deeply unsettled mind. Never mind the credibility criteria: what about that mantra of cognitive behavioural therapy: where's the evidence?

By this time Othello's cry of "O misery!" shows that he is totally hooked on the bait. Although there is a desperate rally, where he says that he'll really believe when he sees evidence: "I'll see before I doubt; when I doubt, prove", the fact that he's even having this conversation allows for the possibility that Desdemona is unfaithful. Iago is quick to move on this "I speak not yet of proof." And what does "yet" imply? That there will be some.

Next, the masterstroke: "She did deceive her father, marrying you". The emphasis is on deception, not on the fact that she loved him so much that she was prepared to deceive her father. Iago is using a disanalogy: that her father loved and trusted her as Othello loves and trusts her. She deceived her father, therefore she will deceive Othello.

There is yet more in this scene to show us how brilliantly Iago plays the insecure, vulnerable Othello, the Othello who was just waiting for this to happen, so that he could stop fearing it, the Othello who lives in the man's world of warfare where trusting one's comrades is at least as important as is trusting one's wife. There is a clear echo of *Much Ado About Nothing* here, but when I first looked at *Othello* in this way I was hardly on the nursery slopes of the critical thinking range. I knew that Iago was doing something to subvert reason while yet somehow cloaking himself in it. I could see how plausible his apparent argument was, and how little chance Othello had to resist its seduction. At the time I didn't know how to express this and thus I realised that I really did need to learn more about this critical thinking stuff in order to understand the structures and the moves and to be able to name them and attune myself to identifying them. The rest is history!

Iago   *Mark me with what violence she first loved the Moor, but for bragging, and telling her fantastical lies. Love him still for prating? Let not thy discreet heart think it. Her eye must be fed; and what delight shall she have to look on the devil? When the blood is made dull with the act of sport, there should be, again to inflame it and give satiety a fresh appetite, loveliness in favour, sympathy in years, manners, and beauties: all of which the Moor is defective in. Now for want of these required conveniences, her delicate tenderness will find itself abused, begin to heave the gorge, disrelish and abhor the Moor; very nature will instruct her in it; and compel her to some second choice. Now sir, this granted – as it is a most pregnant and unforced position – who stands so eminent in the degree of this fortune as Cassio does, a knave very voluble, no further conscionable than in putting on the mere form of civil and humane seeming, for the better compassing of his salt and most hidden loose affection? Why, none; why, none. A slipper and subtle knave, a finder of occasions; that has an eye can stamp and counterfeit advantages, though true advantage never present itself; a devilish knave. Beside, the knave is handsome, young and hath all those requisites in him that folly and green minds look after. A pestilent complete knave; and the woman hath found him already.*

Roderigo   *I cannot believe that in her; she's full of most blessed condition.*

Iago   *Blessed fig's end! The wine she drinks is made of grapes. If she had been blessed, she would never have loved the Moor. Blessed pudding! Didst though not see her paddle with the palm of his hand? Didst not mark that?*

Roderigo   *Yes, that I did, but that was but courtesy.*

Iago   *Lechery, by this hand …*

II (1) 21 /tt

Othello   *Excellent wretch! Perdition catch my soul*
But I do love thee; and when I love thee not,
Chaos is come again.

Iago   *My noble lord –*

Othello   *What dost thou say, Iago?*

Iago   *Did Michael Cassio, when you wooed my lady,*
Know of your love?

Othello   *He did, from first to last. Why dost thou ask?*

Iago   *But for a satisfaction of my thought;*
No further harm.

Othello   *Why of thy thought, Iago?*

Iago   *I did not think he had been acquainted with her.*

Othello   *Oh yes, and went between us very oft.*

Iago   *Indeed?*

Othello   *Indeed? Ay, indeed. Discern'st thou aught in that?*
Is he not honest?

Iago   *Honest, my lord?*

Othello   *Honest? Ay, honest.*

Iago   *My lord, for aught I know.*

Othello   *What dost thou think?*

Iago   *Think, my lord?*

Othello   *Think, my lord? Alas, thou echoest me,*

As if there were some monster in thy thought
Too hideous to be shown. Thou dost mean something.
I heard thee say even now, thou lik'st not that,
When Cassio left my wife. What didst not like?
And when I told thee he was of my counsel
In my whole course of wooing, thou cried'st 'Indeed?'
And didst contract and purse thy brow together,
As if thou then hadst shut up in thy brain
Some horrible conceit. If thou dost love me,
Show me thy thought.

Iago   *My lord, you know I love you.*

Othello   *I think thou dost.*
And for I know thou'rt full of love and honesty,
And weigh'st thy words before thou giv'st them breath,
Therefore these stops of thine affright me more.
For such things in a false disloyal knave
Are tricks of custom; but in a man that's just
They're close dilations, working from the heart,
That passion cannot rule.

Iago   *For Michael Cassio,*
I dare be sworn I think that he is honest.

Othello   *I think so too.*

Iago   *Men should be what they seem;*
Or those that be not, would they might seem none.

Othello   *Certain, men should be what they seem.*

Iago   *Why then, I think Cassio's an honest man.*

Othello   *Nay, yet there's more in this.*
I prithee speak to me as to thy thinkings,
As thou dost ruminate, and give thy worst of thoughts
The worst of words.

Iago   *Good my lord, pardon me.*
Thou I am bound to every act of duty,
I am not bound to that all slaves are free to.
Utter my thoughts? Why, say they are vile and false?
As where's that palace whereinto foul things
Sometimes intrude not? Who has a breast so pure,
But some uncleanly apprehensions
Keep lects and law-days, and in session sit
With meditations lawful?

Othello   *Thou dost conspire against thy friend, Iago,*
If thou but think'st him wronged, and mak'st his ear
A stranger to thy thoughts.

Iago   *I do beseech you,*
Though I perchance am vicious in my guess –
As I confess it is my nature's plague
To spy into abuses, and oft my jealousy
Shapes faults that are not – that your wisdom,
From one that so imperfectly conceits,
Would take no notice, nor build yourself a trouble
Out of his scattering and unsure observance.
It were not for your quiet nor your good,
Nor for my manhood, honesty, wisdom,
To let you know my thoughts.

Othello   *What dost thou mean?*

Iago   *Good name in man and woman, dear my lord,*
Is the immediate jewel of their souls.
Who steals my purse, steals trash; 'tis something, nothing;
'Twas mine, 'tis his, and has been slave to thousands;
But he that filches from me my good name
Robs me of that which not enriches him,
And makes me poor indeed.

Othello   *By heaven, I'll know thy thoughts.*

Iago   *You cannot, if my heart were in your hand,*
Nor shall not, whilst 'tis in my custody.

Othello   *Ha!*

Iago   *O beware my lord of jealousy;*
It is the green-eyed monster which doth mock
The meat it feeds on. That cuckold lives in bliss
Who certain of his fate loves not his wronger,
But O, what damned minutes tells he o'er
Who dotes, yet doubts, suspects, yet fondly loves.

Othello   *O misery!*

Iago   *Poor and content is rich, and rich enough;*
But riches fineless is as poor as winter
To him that ever fears he shall be poor.
Good God, the souls of all my tribes defend
From jealousy!

Othello   *Why, why is this?*
Think'st thou I'd make a life of jealousy,
To follow still the changes of the moon
With fresh suspicions? No, to be once in doubt
Is once to be resolved. Exchange me for a goat,
When I shall turn the business of my soul
To such exsufflicate and blown surmises,
Matching thy inference. 'Tis not to make me jealous
To say my wife is fair, feeds well, loves company,
Is free of speech, sings, plays, and dances well;
Where virtue is, these are more virtuous.
Nor from mine own weak merits will I draw
The smallest fear or doubt of her revolt,
For she had eyes, and chose me. No, Iago,
I'll see before I doubt; when I doubt, prove;
And on the proof, there is no more but this –
Away at once with love or jealousy.

Iago   I am glad of this; for now I shall have reason
         To show the love and duty that I bear you
         With franker spirit. Therefore, as I am bound,
         Receive it from me. I speak not yet of proof.
         Look to your wife; observe her well with Cassio;
         Wear your eyes thus, not jealous nor secure.
         I would not have your free and noble nature,
         Out of self-bounty, be abused. Look to't.
         I know our country dispositions well;
         In Venice they do let God see the pranks
         They dare not show their husbands; their best conscience
         Is not to leave't undone, but keep't unknown.

Othello   Dost thou say so?

Iago   She did deceive her father, marrying you;
         And when she seemed to shake, and fear your looks,
         She loved them most.

Othello   And so she did.

Iago   Why, go to then;
         She that so young could give out such a seeming,
         To seel her father's eyes up close as oak –
         He thought 'twas witchcraft – but I am much to blame;
         I humbly do beseech you of your pardon
         For too much loving you.

Othello   I am bound to thee for ever.

Iago   I see this hath a little dashed your spirits.

Othello   Not a jot, not a jot.

Iago   I'faith, I fear it has.
         I hope you will consider what is spoke
         Comes from my love. But I do see y'are moved.
         I am to pray you not to strain my speech

To grosser issues, nor to the larger reach
Than to suspicion.

Othello *I will not.*

Iago *Should you do so my lord,*
My speech should fall into such vile success
Which my thoughts aimed not. Cassio's my worthy friend –
My lord, I see y'are moved.

Othello *No, not much moved.*
I do not think but Desdemona's honest.

Iago *Long live she so. And long live you to think so.*

Othello *And yet, how nature erring from itself –*

Iago *Ay, there's the point: as, to be bold with you,*
Not to affect many proposed matches
Of her own clime, complexion and degree,
Whereto we see in all things nature tends.
Foh! One may smell in such a will most rank,
Foul disproportion, thoughts unnatural.
But pardon me, I do not in position
Distinctly speak of her, though I may fear
Her will, recoiling to her better judgement,
May fall to match you with her country forms,
And happily repent.

Othello *Farewell, farewell.*
If more thou dost perceive, let me know more.
Set on thy wife to observe. Leave me, Iago.

Iago [Going] *My lord, I take my leave.*

Othello *Why did I marry? This honest creature doubtless*
Sees and knows more, much more, than he unfolds.

Iago   [Returns] *My lord, I would I might entreat your honour*
To scan this thing no further. Leave it to time.
Although 'tis fit that Cassio have his place,
For sure he fills it up with great ability,
Yet if you please to hold him off awhile,
You shall by that perceive him and his means.
Note if your lady strain his entertainment
With any strong or vehement importunity;
Much will be seen in that. In the meantime,
Let me be thought too busy in my fears,
As worthy cause I have to fear I am,
And hold her free, I do beseech your honour.

Othello   *Fear not my government.*

Iago   *I once more take my leave.*   [Exit]

III (iii) 90–256

2
Measure for Measure

She hath prosperous art
When she will play with reason and discourse,
And well she can persuade.

I have those lines from *Measure for Measure* up on my classroom wall, as a complement to all the other reasons for studying critical thinking. They sit alongside *Critical Thinkers never die … they just come to a conclusion*, which was the only printable entry in the Christmas slogan competition for my students.

Known as a "problem play", *Measure for Measure* is often perplexing and sometimes disconcerting. Good people do bad things; other good people have bad things done to them. But where the great tragedies get us close to characters with whom we can empathise, at its most extreme reading we have no one in this play to like or even care about. The "romantic interest" of Claudio and Juliet is as peripheral as are Rosencrantz and Guildenstern to *Hamlet* and, just like them, the two hapless lovers serve as mere plot devices for most of the time. The leading man is deeply unsympathetic and 21st century readers find the leading woman difficult to say the least. Although looking at what was happening in England at the time in which the play was written can help students appreciate why Shakespeare wrote it as he did, it doesn't make them like Isabella any the more. Always a challenge to teach, in terms of engaging students, treating it as a critical thinking exercise seems to make our involvement with it so much more rigorous, detailed and rewarding. It focuses us on language, but not with the exclusively stylistic approach which we might hitherto have used. It reinforces our appreciation of the writer and it gives a methodology for analysis which students find amenable.

The Duke of Vienna has left his city in the charge of Angelo, "a man whose blood / Is very snow-broth". His job is to clean up the town, the lax morality of which the Duke has failed to control. Angelo goes by the letter of the law; one of his unfortunate victims, still living by the old ways, is Claudio, who has got his betrothed, Juliet, pregnant. The penalty for this evident fornication: death. Claudio's only hope lies in the persuasive powers of his sister, who has just entered a convent. Can her purity, her lack of guile and her capacity for reasoning come to his rescue?

First, though, let's cast our critical thinking eye on the Duke's justification for what he has done.

It goes something like this:

I have for a long time let people get away with not obeying the law.
This needs sorting out.
I can't sort it out because:
  a) I would thereby be acting inconsistently;
  b) the people would hate me.
Therefore I've given the job to Angelo.

We learn in critical thinking that "therefore" signals a conclusion, but that it can also be deceiving. How often do we find "therefore" simply disguising something which clearly isn't supported by any reasons! In critical thinking we call this a "spurious therefore", which signals either sloppy thinking or is a rhetorical device which deliberately disguises an assertion as a conclusion.

And before we get to that, is there not an assumption in this "argument"?: an unstated reason which must be assumed if the argument is to work. The assumption comes between the first and second sentences, and is that the laws were good ones – that is, just ones. But were they? Because this reason isn't stated, the friar doesn't challenge it; likewise, a reader not wearing the antennae of the critical thinker might overlook it too – and yet it's a key point in the whole play, for if the law is unjust then Claudio should not be condemned, and Isabella would not be compromised by Angelo. It seems that the Duke, rather than reflecting upon the laws, has merely made the assumption that liberality is a bad thing.

So, why did he leave Angelo in charge?

People are getting away with not obeying the laws.
(This is a bad thing, because the laws are good.)
Therefore this needs sorting out.
I couldn't do it myself because that would be inconsistent and the people
would hate me for being thus.
Therefore I have appointed Angelo.

Is it an argument? Or an explanation? And what's the difference?

It's very easy to mistake an explanation for an argument, especially as
explanations can contain argument indicators such as "therefore" and
"because"; they might even say, "For the following reasons ..." or "There are
three reasons why ...". The Duke's justification for leaving Angelo in charge
in Vienna looks at first reading, sounds at first hearing, very much like an
argument. In an argument the conclusion is something that the "author" of the
argument wants the reader or listener to accept, be persuaded of or do. The
greater the change required in our thinking, the more compelling must be the
reasons, to the point at which if we accept the reasons we must accept the
conclusion – and we have a valid argument. An explanation, on the other
hand, tells us why something is so, or why something is true. That last
sentence was an explanation. If you were to dispute my use of the word I
might have to come up with an argument as to why you should accept it.

An explanation tells us what, how or why, without trying to persuade us to
accept something or to change our minds. The Duke's words to the friar in
I (iii) ll 12 – 55 seem like an uncontentious explanation; uncontentious, until
we realise that it might not be an explanation masquerading as an argument,
but the reverse. He knows that the friar is dubious about what he, the Duke,
has done, and although he speaks as if he doesn't need to do any persuading,
he does, and he is: he's trying to persuade the friar to accept the conclusion:
"And this is a good thing", which is the actual conclusion of the argument.

Instead of reading this within the text as a rather long-winded justification for
a rather questionable decision by a man we're not really very interested in, by
marking it up as an argument we are not only getting close to the text; we are
getting close to the mind of the Duke and to one of the key issues of the play,
that is, are the laws just?

After this, the Duke needs to persuade the friar to help him disguise himself, in order that he might spy on his people. Does he use an argument here? Or even an explanation pretending argument? No: he reverts to an appeal to authority. That is, you will do this not because I have persuaded you through reasoning that it should be done, but because I am more powerful than you are. There is a nice irony here: I, who am using my power to do this, have abnegated my power to another, and wish to appear as someone without power – although with authority.

Here we have the Duke using argument to justify what appears a very odd decision, and doing it cleverly and, in the Shakespearian sense, subtly; we have learned a lot about him – much more than just what it is he's done. The consequences of his actions are about to unfold to us, as we meet Angelo.

In our first encounter with Angelo he is trying to justify his strict adherence to the law to the more pragmatic Escalus:

We must not make a scarecrow of the law,
Setting it up to fear the birds of prey,
And let it keep one shape till custom make it
Their perch and not their terror.

If this is an argument, it too makes the assumption that the law is good; for, clearly, if it is bad, it *should* be made a scarecrow. But Angelo never questions this, and this is part of his character.

Escalus, however, wants to persuade Angelo to change his mind. Unfortunately for Claudio, he isn't very good at it. What "reasons" does he give to support his conclusion that Angelo should save Claudio? That Claudio had a noble father. Is this relevant? That Angelo might have done the same thing in Claudio's place. Equally irrelevant. If something is wrong, it neither matters how well placed the perpetrator is, nor whether his crime might tempt others. The latter is a *tu quoque* fallacy: you can't get me for doing this, because you are doing it / everyone else is doing it. (This is very useful in teaching. Whenever I point out some minor misdemeanour to critical thinking students and they say – well, s/he was doing it, I simply raise my eyebrows and the others say: "*Tu quoque*: that's not an argument!" What I haven't yet worked out is, why it's only critical thinking students who commit misdemeanours in the first place.)

Unsurprisingly, given this absence of reasoned argument, Angelo is not persuaded to change his mind: Claudio must die – Claudio's only hope, then lies with Isabella.

Isabella goes to plead with Angelo, and is careful to establish her credentials at the outset:

There is a vice that most I do abhor,
And most desire should meet the blow of justice;
For which I would not plead, but that I must,
For which I must not plead, but that I am
At war 'twixt will and will not.

Straight away Shakespeare gives her a control over language and reasoning which makes us listen a little more attentively. She takes a gamble, in emphasising the wickedness of the offence, thus showing Angelo that she, like him, is a person for whom morality is paramount. However, she justifies her coming to plead for clemency not through broken rhythms and fragmented rhymes, but through a balanced and indeed perfectly symmetrical pair of lines; but then the enjambment from the fourth to the fifth alters the rhythmic, semantic and syntactic balance, exposing the tension she is experiencing between what she ought to believe and what she has been asked to do.

Her next gambit is to ask that the fault remain condemned, but that the perpetrator might not be.

Angelo is very quick to show the illogicality of this:

Condemn the fault, and not the actor of It …?

Although her suggestion is not as absurd as Angelo suggests: by detaching the "crime" from the "criminal", or the minor misdemeanour from the student, are we not working towards restorative practice? This is itself an interesting forum for debate with students. A film which works here, incidentally, is

Minority Report, where the authorities arrest those who have been envisioned, by seers, committing future crimes. At their point of arrest they have not actually done anything. The procedure has prevented a crime – good – but they are still treated as criminals.

Isabella appears to give up at this point, perhaps less robust in her arguing than our contemporary students would hope (but then they do find it difficult to understand such personal and public repugnance against fornication).

The rakish Lucio, though, tells her to keep going, although the method he suggests is not Isabella's:

> ... *entreat him,*
> *Kneel down before him, hang upon his gown* ...

No, not her style. She offers an idea instead:

> ... *I do think that you might pardon him,*
> *And neither heaven nor man grieve at the mercy.*

Interestingly, Angelo doesn't express any curiosity about how this might be achieved. He doesn't enquire as to her reasons for saying this, but tries to end the debate with an appeal to authority:

> *I will not do't*

Cleverly, she takes this and uses it against him:

> *But can you if you would?*

There is a nice distinction here: if he had the will to, if he chose to, would it be possible? Is it in his power? This is, by accident or design, a key to Angelo: he is in borrowed robes and as such he is over zealous in his exploitation of the power he has been given.

He replies, "Look what I will not, that I cannot do."

She pursues this: "But might you do't, and do the world no wrong ..."

Again, the appeal to authority: "He's sentenced, 'tis too late."

Isabella manages to challenge this too:

> *Too late? Why no; I that do speak a word*
> *May call it again.*

The implication of this is, and who am I? No-one. You, however, have the power to recall even powerful words such as those which condemn a man to death.

She continues to suggest that the more powerful a person is, the more potent is their use of mercy. She also tries a little hypothetical reasoning, suggesting, as did Escalus, that had the roles been reversed, Claudio would have shown mercy. Perhaps she wishes that Angelo had to make his decision behind John Rawls' "veil of ignorance". Behind this veil we make choices without knowing who we are, or would be. There can be no self-interest in the decision: Angelo would have to consider the possibility that he might be a person who has done what Claudio has done. Would his judgement still be the same?

Reading this as a critical thinker (as well as a student of literature) gets us close to characters and especially to Isabella, who is one of Shakespeare's articulate women here in the unique position, as a novitiate, of not overtly using feminine wiles to get her way. Indeed, this understanding enhances our response to the interaction of Angelo and Isabella, as we attune to the highly charged sexuality of the verbal fencing which is taking place.

Angelo, as yet, has still failed to respond rationally to her arguments – here's that appeal to authority again, only now, "It is the law, not I, condemn your brother".

Claudio is to die the next day; Isabella responds to this with an attempt at argument by analogy. Just as we only kill fowl at an appropriate time, we should only kill Claudio at an appropriate time. We show respect to our digestion by waiting and we should show respect to heaven by waiting. This is a hopeless analogy, based on so few similarities and so many dissimilarities that it is a complete disanalogy.

Angelo eschews her call for pity by saying that showing justice *is* showing pity. This point might warrant a discussion on the different definitions of justice and pity which occur throughout the play, and how important it is that all cohabitants of a civic society understand the same by such terms.

Isabella continues, first at the same time appearing to flatter him – "Oh, it is excellent / To have a giant's strength" and then suggesting that the really strong don't have to show their strength: "but it is tyrannous / To use it like a giant …". And so on, until Angelo discloses in an aside that Claudio's words have, indeed proved true: her "prosperous art" appears to be having a powerful effect:

> *She speaks, and 'tis such sense*
> *That my sense breeds with it.*

Here critical thinkers and literature students will converge in their understanding of the ambiguous use of the word sense!

Thus, he asks her to return the next day, for more of the same.

Let us turn now to Act II, scene iv, line 30 ff.

It doesn't start well for Isabella. "Your brother cannot live"; "he must die" seem pretty conclusive, but Isabella is canny enough to ask, "Under your sentence?" Because she knows that we must all die, but won't accept that there's only one way in which Claudio can. Angelo tries an analogy.

A good analogy needs the similarities to be many, or strong, or both.

Pardoning Claudio for fornication is like pardoning a murderer. Now, before we go further with this, ask students how this might be? Can they construct an analogy which would be strong?

In what ways are the *acts of pardoning* similar? Or is it that the two *offences* are similar?

Taking away a life through breaking the law is as "easy" as to *create* a life through breaking the law. Murder is stealing something already made; fornication (or "saucy sweetness") is counterfeiting coins (i.e. people). Eh?

After this outrageous attempt at argument by analogy Angelo comes clean (or rather, dirty), and presents Isabella with a false dilemma, a false dichotomy: only if you sleep with me will your brother live. Why is it false? Because there are other ways of saving Claudio, we want to say.

If A (you sleep with me) then B (Claudio lives)
Not A (you don't)
So, not B (he doesn't)

This is denying the antecedent, as critical thinking students would say, and it's invalid.

But given Angelo's absolute power in this case, it's not in *practice* false: there *is* no alternative:

> *Admit no other way to save his life …*
> *Either*
> *You must lay down the treasures of your body*
> *… or else to let him suffer.*

Cunningly, this is all couched in hypothesis, a kind of cowardly mind experiment: "Finding yourself desired of such a person … What would you do?"

How can Isabella fight back now? (Of course, most of the students don't see it as a problem – they can't weigh chastity against a life in the same way that Isabella does.) What does she do? She uses the very authority and power which Angelo is wielding over her.

He's said, either you sleep with me or Claudio dies; she counters with, either you pardon him or I'll tell everyone about you.

Naturally, Angelo just comes up with another appeal to authority, and perhaps fear – no-one will believe you: "Say what you can, my false o'erweighs your true."

This leaves Isabella on the stage, her thoughts expressed aloud for us to hear. What should she do? She concludes that all she can do is to prepare her brother for his death. "More than our brother is our chastity" is a very difficult one for some contemporary students, and we have to take a historicist side step here, as well as working through some of our ethical theories from A level critical thinking. (For Isabella, Divine Command overrides everything, and this seems to be far more difficult for students to understand than the notion that Henry V had a "right" to invade France.)

Of course, things work out in the end, but not before the Duke himself falls prey to Isabella's irresistible mixture of qualities. He seems to derive great pleasure from putting her in a dire situation towards the end of the play, giving the public to understand that he does not believe her. He is like a man entranced by the physical suppleness of a limbo dancer, continually lowering the bar so that she has to use more and more of her arguing skills.

The conclusion drawn by the second year A level literature students with whom I worked through the many arguments in *Measure for Measure* was that it was a "really good" way of doing it and that they "understood the play a lot better" after we had done so. They'd acquired a useful set of tools for analysis as well, and a mini glossary of terms which they began to use with confidence in their discussions and essays. It didn't make them like Isabella any more, but at least they conceded that she was clever!

After this, the students engaged in debate, taking sides either for or against Isabella and the Duke. They were allocated one of the characters and had to support their conclusion with reasons. Here are the reasons which I recorded as they were debating:

We should condemn Isabella because:
- she effectively condemns her brother to death;
- Juliet would have no husband and the child no father;
- she is hiding behind religion;
- she is tangled in a web of lies;
- she expresses no relief on discovering that Claudio is alive;
- she "goes off with" the Duke, after all her talk of chastity (at least, she makes no protest);
- she is naive in thinking that Angelo could be so easily deflected.

We should not condemn Isabella because:

- there is no evidence that she "goes off with" the Duke;
- she herself could have become pregnant (by Angelo);
- Marianna does want to sleep with Angelo;
- if she slept with him her own life would be ruined;
- she's a victim of this mess;
- she loves her brother, believes in God and genuinely believes that her brother will be going to a better place;
- she did at least try and fight for him, despite her beliefs;
- we must consider the culture of the time: she shouldn't have to give up her right to chastity;
- she has no guarantee that Angelo would honour his agreement: she knows he can change his mind;
- we know nothing of the relationship between Isabella and Claudio prior to this.

We should condemn the Duke because:

- handing over his authority is cowardly, hypocritical, wanting to have his cake and eat it;
- he uses religion as a shield, taking advantage of people's trust in the church;
- he subverts the religious power people think is invested in him: he can't absolve anyone and so he indirectly condemns them;
- his actions are not thought through; they are rash and he hasn't considered the possible consequences;
- he's protecting Isabella's virginity for himself;
- he proposes marriage to a nun;
- he betrays Lucio's trust – it was virtually entrapment, but he punishes Lucio just the same;
- he is scheming and manipulative;
- although all's well in the end, he just got lucky;

- he uses emotional blackmail;
- if what Lucio says is true, then he is even more of a hypocrite;
- if his plan had gone wrong, what of Marianna?
- he prolongs the agony at the end;
- Isabella and Marianna are publicly humiliated;
- he tells Isabella that Claudio is dead;
- he's a sadist, entertained by the anguish of others.

We should not condemn the Duke because:

- he has a good reason to hand over his authority;
- his actions will be for the good of the state;
- he admits his mistakes and takes action;
- regarding religion: a monarch is closer to God than a friar (but he's not a monarch) (but he is a Duke …);
- he knew that the bed trick couldn't fail to benefit Marianna, because in the end he would rule on it;
- the deception involving her isn't to benefit himself;
- he is aware of his error in appointing Angelo, but what happened couldn't have been anticipated;
- he learns from his mistakes and encourages others to do so;
- rather than betraying Lucio's trust, he needs to know how he is viewed; it's not his fault that Lucio puts his foot in it. Lucio is not a good person, and Lucio shouldn't trust anyone;
- he believes in the principle of going through pain in order to emerge the stronger;
- he could have had Lucio killed, but doesn't;
- everybody gets a second chance;
- his plan is clever – Juliet, Isabella, and Marianna benefit, as well as Claudio;
- he saves Claudio.

These initial "reasons" needed to be refined, challenged, expanded upon, but showed great engagement with the text, extensive understanding of the characters and issues, and paved the way for some excellent essays. Those essays, of course, looked at how Shakespeare *presents* the characters, and students looked at all the things that literature students do look at, but underpinning their analysis of language, structure and form was a very strong sense of exactly what the issues were. This was particularly relevant to the style of question they had to answer in the exam, which put forward two opposing views of any given character, or theme, and invited students to engage in an informed debate and to draw their own conclusion. Does this sound familiar?

Duke   *I have deliver'd to Lord Angelo,*
A man of stricture and firm abstinence,
My absolute power and place here in Vienna,
And he supposes me travell'd to Poland;
For so I have strew'd it in the common ear,
And so it is received. Now, pious sir,
You will demand of me why I do this.

Friar Thomas
Gladly, my lord.

Duke   *We have strict statutes and most biting laws,*
The needful bits and curbs to headstrong weeds,
Which for this fourteen years we have let slip,
Even like an o'ergrown lion in a cave
That goes out not to prey. Now, as fond fathers
Having bound up the threatening twigs of birch
Only to stick it in their children's sight
For terror, not to use – in time the rod
More mocked than feared – so our decrees,
Dead to infliction, to themselves are dead,
And Liberty plucks Justice by the nose,
The baby beats the nurse, and quite athwart
Goes all decorum.

Friar Thomas

> *It rested in your grace*
> *To unloose this tied-up justice when you pleased,*
> *And it in you more dreadful would have seem'd*
> *Than in Lord Angelo.*

Duke   *I do fear, too dreadful:*
> *Sith 'twas my fault to give the people scope,*
> *'Twould be my tyranny to strike and gall them*
> *For what I bid them do: for we bid this be done,*
> *When evil deeds have their permissive pass*
> *And not the punishment. Therefore indeed, my father,*
> *I have on Angelo imposed the office;*
> *Who may in th'ambush of my name strike home,*
> *And yet my nature never in the fight*
> *To do in slander. And to behold his sway,*
> *I will, as 'twere a brother of your order,*
> *Visit both prince and people: therefore, I prithee,*
> *Supply me with the habit and instruct me*
> *How I may formally in person bear me*
> *Like a true friar. More reasons for this action*
> *At our more leisure shall I render you;*
> *Only, this one: Lord Angelo is precise;*
> *Stands at a guard with envy; scarce confesses*
> *That his blood flows, or that his appetite*
> *Is more to bread than stone: hence shall we see,*
> *If power change purpose, what our seemers be.*

I (iii) 12–55

Angelo   *We must not make a scarecrow of the law,*
> *Setting it up to fear the birds of prey,*
> *And let it keep one shape till custom make it*
> *Their perch and not their terror.*

Escalus *Ay, but yet*
> *Let us be keen, and rather cut a little,*

Than fall, and bruise to death. Alas, this gentleman,
Whom I would save, had a most noble father!
Let but your honour know,
Whom I believe to be most strait in virtue,
That, in the working of your own affections,
Had time cohered with place or place with wishing,
Or that the resolute acting of your blood
Could have attain'd the effect of your own purpose,
Whether you had not sometime in your life
Err'd in this point which now you censure him,
And pull'd the law upon you.

Angelo   *'Tis one thing to be tempted, Escalus,*
Another thing to fall. I not deny,
The jury, passing on the prisoner's life,
May in the sworn twelve have a thief or two
Guiltier than him they try. What's open made to justice,
That justice seizes: what knows the laws
That thieves do pass on thieves? 'Tis very pregnant,
The jewel that we find, we stoop and take't
Because we see it; but what we do not see
We tread upon, and never think of it.
You may not so extenuate his offence
For I have had such faults; but rather tell me,
When I, that censure him, do so offend,
Let mine own judgement pattern out my death,
And nothing come in partial. Sir, he must die.

II (i) 1–31

Isabella *There is a vice that most I do abhor,*
And most desire should meet the blow of justice;
For which I would not plead, but that I must,
For which I must not plead, but that I am
At war 'twixt will and will not.

Angelo   *Well: the matter?*

Isabella   *I have a brother is condemn'd to die:*
I do beseech you, let it be his fault,
And not my brother.

…

Angelo   *Condemn the fault and not the actor of it?*
Why, every fault's condemn'd ere it be done:
Mine were the very cipher of a function,
To fine the faults whose fine stands in record,
And let go by the actor.

…

Isabella   *Must he needs die?*

Angelo   *Maiden, no remedy.*

Isabella   *Yes, I do think that you might pardon him,*
And neither heaven nor man grieve at the mercy.

Angelo   *I will not do't.*

Isabella   *But can you, if you would?*

Angelo   *Look, what I will not, that I cannot do.*

Isabella   *But might you do't, and do the world no wrong,*
If so your heart were touch'd with that remorse
As mine is to him?

Angelo   *He's sentenced; 'tis too late.*

…

Isabella   *Too late? why, no: I that do speak a word,*
May call it back again. Well, believe this,
No ceremony that to great ones 'longs,

Not the king's crown, nor the deputed sword,
The marshal's truncheon, nor the judge's robe,
Becomes them with one half so good a grace
As mercy does.
If he had been you and you as he,
You would have slipt like him; but he, like you,
Would not have been so stern.

Angelo *Pray you, begone.*

Isabella *I pray to heaven I had your potency,*
And you were Isabel! should it then be thus?
No; I would tell what 'twere to be a judge,
And what a prisoner.

 ...

Angelo *Your brother is a forfeit of the law,*
And you but waste your words.

Isabella *Alas, alas!*
Why, all the souls that were were forfeit once;
And He that might the vantage best have took
Found out the remedy. How would you be,
If He, which is the top of judgement, should
But judge you as you are? O, think on that;
And mercy then will breathe within your lips,
Like man new made.

Angelo *Be you content, fair maid;*
It is the law, not I condemn your brother:
Were he my kinsman, brother, or my son,
It should be thus with him: he must die tomorrow.

Isabella *Tomorrow! O, that's sudden! Spare him, spare him!*
He's mot prepared for death. Even for our kitchens
We kill the fowl of season: shall we serve heaven

With less respect than we do minister
To our gross selves? Good, good my lord, bethink you;
Who is it that hath died for this offence?
There's many have committed it.

...

Angelo   *The law hath not been dead, though it hath slept:*
Those many had not dared to do that evil,
If the first that did the edict infringe
Had answer'd for his deed: now, 'tis awake,
Takes note of what is done; and, like a prophet,
Looks in a glass, that shows what future evils,
Either new, or by remises new-conceived,
And so in progress to be hatch'd and born,
Are now to have no successive degrees,
But, ere they live, to end.

Isabella   *Yet show some pity*

Angelo   *I show it most of all when I show justice;*
For then I pity those I do not know,
Which a dismiss'd offence would after gall;
And do him right that, answering one foul wrong,
Lives not to act another. Be satisfied;
Your brother dies tomorrow; be content.

Isabella   *So you must be the first that gives this sentence,*
And he, that suffers. O, it is excellent
To have a giant's strength; but it is tyrannous
To use it like a giant.

...

Isabella   *Could great men thunder*
As Jove himself does, Jove would ne'er be quiet,
For every pelting, petty officer
Would use his heaven for thunder;

Nothing but thunder! Merciful Heaven,
Thou rather with thy sharp and sulphurous bolt
Split'st the unwedgeable and gnarled oak
Than the soft myrtle: but man, proud man,
Drest in a little brief authority,
Most ignorant of what he's most assured,
His glassy essence, like an angry ape,
Plays such fantastic tricks before high heaven
As make the angels weep; who, with our spleens,
Would all themselves laugh mortal.

...

Isabella *We cannot weigh our brother with ourself;*
Great men may jest with saints; 'tis wit in them,
But in the less foul profanation.

...

Isabella *That in the captain's but a choleric word,*
Which in the soldier is flat blasphemy.

...

Angelo *Why do you put these sayings upon me?*

Isabella *Because authority, though it err like others,*
Hath yet a kind of medicine in itself,
That skins the vice o' the top. Go to your bosom;
Knock there, and ask your heart what it doth know
That's like my brother's fault; if it confess
A natural guiltiness such as is his,
Let it not sound a thought upon your tongue
Against my brother's life.
Angelo [Aside] *She speaks, and 'tis such sense*
That my sense breeds with it.

II (ii) 30–147

Angelo   *... he must die.*

Isabella   *Under your sentence?*

Angelo   *Yea*

Isabella   *When, I beseech you? that in his reprieve,*
    Longer or shorter, he may be so fitted
    That his soul sicken not.

Angelo   *Ha! fie, these filthy vices! It were as good*
    To pardon him that hath from nature stolen
    A man already made, as to remit
    Their saucy sweetness that do coin heaven's image
    In stamps that are forbid; 'tis all as easy
    Falsely to take away a life true made
    As to put metal in restrained means
    To make a false one.

Isabella   *'Tis set down so in heaven, but not in earth.*

Angelo   *Say you so? then I shall pose you quickly.*
    Which had you rather, that the most just law
    Now took your brother's life; or, to redeem him,
    Give up that body to such sweet uncleanness
    As she that he hath stain'd?

Isabella   *Sir, believe this,*
    I had rather give my body than my soul.

Angelo   *I talk not of your soul: our compell'd sins*
    Stand more for number than for accompt.

Isabella   *How say you?*

Angelo   *Nay, I'll not warrant that; for I can speak*
    Against the thing I say. Answer to this:
    I, now the voice of the recorded law,

Pronounce a sentence on your brother's life:
Might there not be a charity in sin
To save this brother's life?

Isabella   *Please you to do't*
I'll take it as a peril to my soul,
It is no sin at all, but charity.

Angelo   *Pleased you to do't at peril of your soul,*
Were equal poise of sin and charity.

Isabella   *That I do beg his life, if it be sin,*
Heaven let me bear it! your granting of my suit,
If that be sin, I'll make it my morn prayer
To have it added to the faults of mine,
And nothing of your answer.

Angelo   *Nay, but hear me.*
Your sense pursues not mine: either you are ignorant,
Or, seem so craftily; and that's not good.

Isabella   *Let me be ignorant, and in nothing good,*
But graciously to know I am no better.

Angelo   *Thus wisdom wishes to appear most bright*
When it doth tax itself; as these black masks
Proclaim an enshield beauty ten times louder
Than beauty could, display'd. But mark me;
To be received plain, I'll speak more gross:
Your brother is to die.

Isabella   *So.*

Angelo   *And his offence is so, as it appears,*
Accountant to the law upon that pain.

Isabella   *True.*

Angelo   *Admit no other way to save his life –*
             As I subscribe not that, nor any other,
             But in the loss of question – that you, his sister,
             Finding yourself desired of such a person,
             Whose credit with the judge, or own great place,
             Could fetch your brother from the manacles
             Of the all-binding law; and that there were
             No earthly mean to save him, but that either
             You must lay down the treasures of your body
             To this supposed, or else to let him suffer:
             What would you do?

Isabella   *As much for my poor brother as myself;*
             That is, were I under terms of death,
             The impression of keen whips I'ld wear as rubies,
             And strip myself to death, as to a bed
             That longing have been sick for, ere I'ld yield
             My body up to shame.

Angelo   *Then must your brother die.*

Isabella   *And 'twere the cheaper way:*
             Better it were a brother died at once,
             Than that a sister, by redeeming him,
             Should die for ever.

Angelo   *Were you not then as cruel as the sentence*
             That you have slander'd so?

Isabella   *Ignominy in ransom and free pardon*
             Are of two houses: lawful mercy
             Is nothing kin to foul redemption.

Angelo   *You seem'd of late to make the law a tyrant;*
             And rather proved the sliding of your brother
             A merriment than a vice.

Isabella   *O, pardon me my lord; it oft falls out,*

To have what we would have, we speak not what we mean:
I something do excuse the thing I hate,
For his advantage that I dearly love.

Angelo   *We are all frail.*

Isabella   *Else let my brother die,*
If not a fedary, but only he
Owe and succeed thy weakness.

Angelo   *Nay, women are frail too.*

Isabella   *Ay, as the glasses where they view themselves;*
Which are as easy broke as they make forms.
Women! Help Heaven! men their creation mar
In profiting by them. Nay, call us ten times frail;
For we are soft as our complexions are,
And credulous to false prints.

Angelo   *I think it well:*
And from this testimony of your own sex –
Since I suppose we are made to be no stronger
Than faults may shake our frames – let me be bold;
I do arrest your words. Be that you are,
That is, a woman; if you be more, you're none;
If you be one, as you are well express'd
By all external warrants, show it now,
By putting on the destined livery.

Isabella   *I have no tongue but one: gentle my lord,*
Let me entreat you speak the former language.

Angelo   *Plainly conceive, I love you.*

Isabella   *My brother did love Juliet,*
And you tell me that he shall die for it.

Angelo   *He shall not, Isabel, if you give me love.*

Isabella   *I know your virtue hath a licence in't,*
Which seems a little fouler than it is,
To pluck on others.

Angelo   *Believe me, on mine honour,*
My words express my purpose.

Isabella   *Ha! little honour to be much believed,*
And most pernicious purpose! Seeming, seeming!
I will proclaim thee, Angelo; look for't:
Sign me a present pardon for my brother,
Or with an outstretch'd throat I'll tell the world aloud
What man thou art.

Angelo   *Who will believe thee, Isabel?*
My unsoil'd name, the austereness of my life,
My vouch against you, and my place i'the state
Will so your accusation overweigh,
That you shall stifle in your own report
And smell of calumny. I have begun,
And now I give my sensual race the rein:
Fit thy consent to my sharp appetite;
Lay by all nicety and prolixious blushes,
That banish what they sue for; redeem thy brother
By yielding up thy body to my will;
Or else he must not only die the death,
But thy unkindness shall his death draw out
To lingering sufferance. Answer me to-morrow,
Or, by the affection that now guides me most,
I'll prove a tyrant to him. As for you,
Say what you can, my false o'erweighs your true.

II (iv) 36–170

3
Much Ado About Nothing

Dishonesty, deception and disguise are never far away in Shakespeare's plays, but whereas characters can never know everything that is going on, we in the audience do. Trickery in the comedies usually adds to our enjoyment; we know that Viola and Rosalind are girls, whereas Olivia and Orlando do not; we know that Olivia is not in love with Malvolio, but that Rosalind is in love with Orlando. We know about the twins in *A Comedy of Errors*, but the characters don't. In the tragedies such trickery can add to our distress, as when we know that Hamlet is doomed through the deception of Claudius and the complicity of Laertes, that Iago is lying and that Juliet isn't dead.

Much Ado About Nothing is a witty comedy but it has a dark heart. Tragedy looms, through deception; but through trickery, tragedy is averted and love discovered. How easily could it have ended thus: through Don John's deception and the credulousness of other characters Hero has to pretend to be dead. For Beatrice, Benedick challenges Claudio to a duel and either or both of them die. On discovering this, either or both of Hero and Beatrice kill themselves. I don't know if anyone's done this with the play, but it would be a powerful feminist revision!

As with *Measure for Measure* and *Othello,* much of the plot rests on deception. Beatrice and Benedick deceive themselves and others in maintaining their dislike of each other; they are deceived in turn by other characters who pretend to each (of Beatrice and Benedick) that the other has declared their love. All is well here, as they really *do* love each other; where the potential tragedy arises is in the plight of the young lovers, Hero and Claudio, being the victims of a cruel trick to make it appear that Hero has sex with another man the night before her wedding. The consequences of this are exacerbated by the fact that the society in which this is depicted is patriarchal,

39

as indeed are the societies in most of Shakespeare's plays and in the great majority of literature written in English until relatively recently. Shakespeare, of course, both highlights and subverts this in his creation of feisty female characters such as Rosalind, Viola and Portia, each of whom dons breeches and enjoys a measure of freedom and independence as a result. In *Much Ado* he holds it up for scrutiny and exposes its foolishness.

There is to be a wedding, a joyous occasion uniting Hero and Claudio. The malevolent Don John, the wicked fairy at the crib, blights this occasion for his own sadistic purposes (although post-Freudian students are willing to suggest that *he* really loves Claudio, or that because he has been replaced in his brother's affections by Claudio he is justified in his distress and subsequent actions: they try to find explanations for his behaviour). Now, the accusation about Hero shouldn't have mattered. There is nothing in Hero which could give rise to such a suspicion being supported, but Don John's sidekick, Borachio, acts out the scene in the hearing of Don Pedro and Claudio, using a gullible substitute.

There is an added irony in that those who believe the slander against Hero include some who fabricated the accounts of romance between Benedick and Beatrice: they seem unable to make any connection between the two situations.

Don John   *Go but with me tonight, and you shall see her chamber window entered, even the night before her wedding day. If you love her then, tomorrow wed her. But it would better fit your honour to change your mind.*

Claudio   *May this be so?*

Don Pedro *I will not think it.*

Don John   *If you dare not trust that you see, confess not that you know. If you will follow me I will show you enough, and when you have seen more and heard more, proceed accordingly.*

Claudio   *If I see anything tonight why I should not marry her, tomorrow, in the congregation where I should wed, then I will shame her.*

Don Pedro   *And as I wooed for thee to obtain her, I will join with thee to*
     disgrace her.

Oh, that they had studied critical thinking and applied credibility criteria!
These are useful as a reminder in any situation where we are being asked to
believe one claim over another as well as where there is no conflict. Some
teachers and textbooks suggest RAVEN as a mnemonic; my students made
this altogether more cool by adding MC, so we have a credibility jock to help
us decide what we should accept as likely to be true.

Does the claimant (Don John) have a **M**otive, either to lie or to tell the truth?
Is there anything which either **C**orroborates or **C**onflicts with a given claim?
(OK, that's two **c**s, but although MCC is memorable for us cricket lovers my
students didn't think that the idea of a big black bird perched on the top of
Father Time at Lord's worked quite as well for them.)

What is the **R**eputation of the claimant? We approach this cautiously, of
course, so as to avoid an *ad hominem* fallacy: we must allow for the
possibility that someone with a reputation for unreliability, or exaggeration,
or even lying could be really telling the truth this time, just like the boy who
cried wolf.
What about the claimant's **A**bility to see or know: do they have unimpeded
eye-witness evidence?
Does the claimant stand to gain financially or in terms of power or status from
their claim being accepted? Do they have a **V**ested interest in a particular
outcome? Again, we must consider that even if they do, their evidence need
not be discounted.
Does the claimant have any *relevant* **E**xpertise?
Finally, is there a likely bias which could account for the emphasis given to
the evidence, or is the claimant **N**eutral?

Obviously, some of these overlap but there are enough (albeit subtle)
differences between them to provide for us a useful checklist to help us in
making our judgements.

What happens when we re-read the tricking of Claudio with these criteria in
mind?

What seems shocking is that Claudio never questions the accusation, despite what he knows of Hero; then his belief is reinforced by the apparent evidence of his eyes and ears. As a result he shames Hero publicly, at the wedding, supported by his comrades and even Hero's father, who is willing to believe his daughter dishonourable on the word of the other men. Leonato has known Hero all her life, and perhaps it is his condemnation of her which the audience finds most disturbing and repugnant. But we've seen it elsewhere in Shakespeare – a father condemning an innocent daughter, with tragic consequences in *King Lear*, or discounting her, as in *The Merchant of Venice* or *Hamlet*.

Let's look first of all at Don John's claim that Hero "is disloyal". This is such an apparently outrageous claim that he *must* support it.

> *The word is too good to paint out her wickedness; I could say she were worse. Think of you any worse title, and I will fit her to it.*

This is simply repeating the claim; as yet no evidence is offered. But, *Go but with me tonight, you shall see and hear her chamber window entered, even the night before her wedding day.*

And Claudio's reaction? "May this be so?" What do we make of this? Of the fact that he doesn't strike down Don John for daring to defame Hero? Don Pedro seems less persuaded: perhaps he is already running through the credibility criteria. But Don John is most persuasive in telling Claudio and Don Pedro that they will see more, and hear more. The fact that he speaks so confidently about this just adds to Claudio's hasty judgement, and he talks of shaming her, and Don Pedro of disgracing her. Avoiding marrying her would be a "plague right well prevented".

Ask your students to apply the criteria:
Does Don John have a motive to lie or to tell the truth?
Is there any corroborative or conflicting evidence?
What is the reputation of the claimant? (And of the accused?)
Does he have the ability to see or know the truth?
Does he have a vested interest in the case going one way rather than another?
Has he any expertise, which gives his claim more weight?
Is he likely to be biased or to be neutral?

Surely in doing this they will conclude that Claudio and Don Pedro are leaping to an ill-judged conclusion, and they will then ask, "What is Shakespeare telling us here?"

Then, what of the physical "evidence" which Claudio thinks he sees? This is tricky, as he *believes* he is seeing Hero with Borachio, and that appears to be that. But why does he believe this? It's dark, they are a distance away – "afar off in the orchard"; he doesn't see her face. And, of course, if he considered Hero's reputation weighed against Don John's, and Don John's likely motive and undoubted vested interest, how could he believe that this is Hero? Even though Borachio is calling out the name Hero, might there not be another explanation for this?

Hero is to be condemned on the basis of Don John's claim and the "eye witnesses", who see in the dark and at a distance(!). Shouldn't the others, especially Leonato, demand good grounds for believing the accusation to be true? How believable is the evidence? How strong? What is the opposing evidence?

Beatrice – alas, only a woman – claims that Hero has been falsely accused; can we apply the credibility criteria to her? She needs a very strong case in order to challenge the "eye witness" account.

What might be *her* motive? Is there anyone to corroborate *her* claim? What is her reputation? Does she have the ability to see or know? Has she a vested interest in one judgement over another? Does she have any relevant expertise? Is she likely to be biased or neutral?

Again, it would be simplistic to simply go through these – and other – criteria and decide that if a character has, for example, a vested interest then that automatically affects the credibility of their evidence. "You would say that, wouldn't you, because you wanted to be a bridesmaid." Suppose she did want to be a bridesmaid; that in itself doesn't make her evidence faulty. Although *we* know that Beatrice is right, looking at the claim and counter claim using the criteria makes it harder to make the judgement in Hero's favour.

Is there anyone in this case who might be neutral? Leonato, Hero's father, might be *expected* to challenge her detractors and support the daughter he has known and loved all her life, as might her cousin and dearest friend Beatrice, so perhaps we might doubt their claims as being biased in favour of Hero (ironic, of course, given Leonato's actual reaction). Don Pedro is highly regarded and has no personal connection with Hero – might we look to him to be neutral? But his loyal comrade Claudio is prepared to believe it of Hero, so can he be disinterested? Should he have been? And, fascinatingly, what of Benedick? He is a comrade of both Claudio and Don Pedro, but knows little of Hero other than the fact that Claudio has fallen in love with her and that Beatrice champions her innocence. Perhaps the only truly neutral observer of these events is the friar, who says,

> *Call me a fool;*
> *Trust not my reading nor my observations …*
> *… Trust not my age*
> *My reverence, my calling, nor divinity,*
> *If this sweet lady lie not guiltless here*
> *Under some biting error.*

Here he is using his own list of criteria to justify why his judgement should be respected.

Is he claiming expertise, perhaps? Relevant expertise, that is. Critical thinking students know that being an expert in one field doesn't mean your claims can be viewed as strong when you are operating in another. If the friar were a good singer or a physician would that make him a more able judge of character? But this is a man who will have been privy to the thoughts of many people in confidence – including, no doubt, Hero. However, we may ask whether this is even a situation in which expertise of any sort is relevant.

What about the criterion of reputation? Look at Don John's and then at Hero's and Beatrice's, for this is what it comes down to in terms of the conflicting claims, which Claudio and the others should consider before making a judgement. It's a tough one, because Claudio and Don Pedro believe they saw and heard the incident, and Leonato has every reason to respect the integrity of the prince. But who forewarned them of it? Don John. And what is his reputation? He is a brooding, embittered, baleful and above all, mistrusted, character, who has to be kept an eye on.

Conrad   *You have of late stood out against your brother, and he has ta'en you newly into his grace; where it is impossible you should take true root but by the fair weather that you make yourself: it is needful that you frame the season for your own harvest.*

Don John   *I had rather be a canker in a hedge than a rose in his grace …*
I am trusted with a muzzle and enfranchised with a clog …
If I had my mouth I would bite …

Hero, on the other hand, has a reputation for honesty and modesty. Don John's jaundiced view of the world, and his history of sibling rebellion might not be enough to make Claudio doubt his word and ascribe any ulterior motive to his part in the disclosure – and anyway, they saw it happen – Hero's reputation, though, was surely one of the things which drew Claudio to her:

Claudio   *Benedick, didst thou note the daughter of Signor Leonato?*

Benedick   *I noted her not; but I looked on her.*

Claudio   *Is she not a modest young lady?*

Her "modesty" – innocence and purity – is the first attribute which Claudio identifies.

However, what makes it so weighted to one side is this. Whatever Hero says, whatever Beatrice says, whatever common sense says, whatever Hero's reputation for goodness and Don John's reputation for badness, this is a man's world and the voices of women are of little account. Hence Beatrice's lament – "Oh God that I were a man! I would eat his heart out in the market-place", and the most dramatic line in the play, when she simply says to Benedick: "Kill Claudio". Now, Benedick does eventually agree to challenge Claudio, but it is clearly not because he has assessed the evidence, but rather because of his newly discovered love for Beatrice, who is not only rallying to the support of someone with whom she is close, but who has assessed the evidence well.

Benedick   *Think you in your soul the Count Claudio hath wronged Hero?*

Beatrice   *Yea, as sure as I have a thought or a soul.*

Benedick   *Enough. I am engaged …*

Thus Benedick prepares to kill Claudio; here is that tragedy in the making, in which perhaps Claudio dies for his foolishness, and Benedick dies for killing a man with no proof of the offence. Disaster is, however, averted, as the painfully loquacious Dogberry and Verges finally manage to collect a confession from Borachio and Conrad and all ends happily.

In working through this aspect of the play using skills borrowed from critical thinking, literature students are reading closely and with a new emphasis. This is rather like changing the activity at the gym: this machine or that set of weights may be targeting the same muscles, but the body seems to become habituated to this over time. A change provides a challenge; a new way of working those areas, just as reading for credibility criteria can give students a whole new way of toning those mental muscles.

4
Credibility and the
First Person Narrator

Picture this: the highest achieving and most aspirational students of English literature and of critical thinking in college on a Saturday to spend a day on narrative, how a story is told. The key text in this case? Christopher Nolan's film *Memento*, and the short story it was based on: Jonathan Nolan's *Memento Mori*.

Memento asks hard questions of its audience, not least of which is "What is going on?" It challenges us to make sense of a story or, rather, to find a story at all; it threatens our need for sequential narrative, and questions the reliability of our only narrator. (Reading *Memento Mori* doesn't necessarily help. It does narrow the options, but we are still left wondering about who is telling us the story and what their relationship to the protagonist is.) To fully explain the value of this film as part of a study of narrative would be to spoil its impact: the learning here must all be experiential! What I can say is that for critical thinkers it asks the following questions:

- What should we believe?
- Why?
- How credible is the evidence which the protagonist, Leonard, believes he is working with? And how credible to us are Leonard, Teddy and Natalie?
- Is there a logic at work in the way the film is organised?
- Can we use logic in trying to make sense of the storyline?

Literature students will probably think about point of view, narrative voice and narrative structure: are these dissimilar from the above? They will look at the way Leonard, as our narrative voice, sees and understands events around him; they will look at how the construct that is the film has organised and re-presented events, and at alternative readings.

The conundrum that is *Memento* is not solved in a single flash of realisation, as is the case with *The Sixth Sense*, for example. Even when we have grasped what's happening with the sequencing of the scenes in black and white and those in colour and have a sense of chronology, we have many unanswered questions and conflicting versions of events. This is another reason why the film is such a good source for learning, as students are encouraged to be speculative, to test hypotheses and compare the credibility of evidence and claims.

Critical thinking students are attuned to reading in a way that is distanced, sceptical and analytical, perhaps to the point of being mechanistic; literature students (and this goes for general readers of novels) are invited to accept the reliability of the first person narrator, the eye which mediates the action for us, and which usually provides the only version of events available to us. There are, of course, interesting exceptions to this in the form of a significant minority of novels with multiple narrators; these narrators, however, are more likely to foreground different interpretations of the same things, rather than insisting on replacing one event with another. *Wuthering Heights* uses multiple narration, but many A level literature novels which use first person narrative will use a single voice which we are invited to trust. The question here is, what can the objective discipline of critical thinking lend to the trustfulness and empathy of the reader of literature? I've rarely known a critical thinking student be *moved* in a lesson by the content of what they are reading, whereas there have been many occasions in literature lessons when I and my students have had to stop reading something which is just making too deep an inroad into our sense of the fragility of the human condition. (This is not to deny, of course, the arresting moments that happen in critical thinking when a student works something out which was hard. There can be joy in the solving of difficulties, and an aesthetic pleasure in the elegance of some students' strategies.) Using critical thinking approaches can never diminish our intimate human relationships with our narrators but it can enable us, through interrogation, to envisage alternative versions of their stories: ironically, a highly imaginative enterprise!

In one sense there's nothing new in this. It's a staple of GCSE teaching to privilege a secondary character (and by implication demote the main protagonists) and explore their point of view, and it has been done famously in *Rosencrantz and Guildenstern are Dead*. But even then, we aren't scrutinising the stories for credibility and logic, or for likelihood, but for character insights.

Kazuo Ishiguro, in *The Remains of the Day*, presents us with a narrator who withholds things from himself and from his readers. The accounts by Stevens give us one impression of himself and of his employer; gradually the reader creates an alternative scenario, in which neither comes out quite as well. For example, there is Stevens' version of an incident involving himself and the housekeeper Mrs Kenton. She has received some distressing news and might have welcomed some words or gestures of affection. Stevens' almost pathological restraint prevents him from acting, but rather than admitting this he creates a scenario which absolves him from doing anything at all. It's almost a straw man, in that he describes something that isn't happening and then uses that as an excuse for his behaviour – in the same way that in an argument someone might put words into the mouth of the opposition and then argue as if they actually were the views of the other person.

As well as the personal, Stevens has to deal with the political, particularly his employer's alleged anti-Semitism. He re-presents history in order to make Lord Darlington (and thereby himself, as Lord Darlington's loyal servant) an admirable figure.

This is tricky, as even Stevens has to recount the fact that Lord Darlington did say, "I've been doing a great deal of thinking, Stevens, a great deal of thinking. And I've reached my conclusion. We cannot have Jews on the staff here at Darlington Hall." The staff at the Hall who are Jews are two housemaids, and so Stevens must go through the housekeeper, Miss Kenton. How will he relate his Lordship's "conclusion" to her, especially since, according to Stevens, "the maids had been perfectly satisfactory employees and – I may as well say that since the Jewish issue has become so sensitive of late – my every instinct opposed the idea of their dismissal." But, "Nevertheless, my duty in this instance was quite clear, and as I saw it, there was nothing to be gained at all in irresponsibly displaying such personal doubts."

Miss Kenton is, unsurprisingly, outraged when Stevens conveys this: how will he deal with it in such a way that he and his employer come out well? Miss Kenton quite properly takes an ethical stance:

> 'Does it not occur to you, Mr Stevens, that to dismiss Ruth and Sarah on these grounds would be simply – wrong? I will not stand for such things. I will not work in a house where such things can occur.'

Stevens continues to put across the line that we do what our employer tells us to do: we are absolved of any responsibility for this decision.

Stevens, we must remember, lives in a time and a culture where loyalty is paramount, and also where there is an assumption that those to whom we owe loyalty know what is for the best. There is an important ethical argument here which critical thinkers would enjoy.

Employing reading and inferential skills to doubt Stevens' account of events or to question his judgement (in which we are helped, of course, by the great skill of the writer) compares usefully with the interpretation of witness accounts and conflicting reports in scenarios used in critical thinking, where in the absence of information and/or knowledge witnesses will speculate upon possibilities and create versions of reality which, while not in any way intended to deceive, could deflect from the possible truth. In addition they might have a motive, especially vested interest, to hide the truth or to replace it with a version more favourable towards themselves, or more advantageous to someone they are trying to protect. English teachers might like to look at examples of past critical thinking papers, in that the scenarios and extracts can provide interesting material to which students can apply the analysis which they would to the exploration of similar situations in literary texts. Another use for these examples is as models for students in creating multiple narratives for novels with first person – and omniscient – narrators in books they are studying. As ever, they will also find invaluable material in Roy van den Brink-Budgen's three critical thinking books.

In critical thinking scenarios we would have multiple conflicting claims; in a first person novel we have a claimant who is unchallenged and in complete control of *what* is presented and the way in which things *are* presented. Writers can, and do, imply doubt, as does Ishiguro; if using an omniscient narrator they may undermine characters through irony, as Jane Austen does so deftly in, for example, *Emma*, as we see in the opening:

Emma Woodhouse, handsome, clever and rich, with a comfortable home and happy disposition, seemed to unite some of the best blessings of existence; and had lived nearly twenty-one years in the world with very little to distress or vex her …

But

The real evils, indeed, of Emma's situation were the power of having rather too much her own way, and a disposition to think a little too well of herself …The danger, however, was at present so unperceived, that they did not by any means rank as misfortunes with her.

Austen undermines her character within the first page, and does so with a remarkably strong word, "evils" to describe Emma's self satisfaction. We subsequently read Emma's character in the light of this, no longer taking her sunny disposition at face value, but now alert to examples of those "evils" coming to the surface.

Ian McEwan's *Enduring Love* has one narrative voice, that of one of the three key characters in the book. So dominant is this that even the chapter devoted to Clarissa's story is a product of Joe's speculative and perhaps self-protecting imagination. When it comes to relying on his version of events involving Jed Parry – including the balloon accident – we have no means of checking the truth of what he is saying. But McEwan gives us plenty of instances where we are encouraged to realise that Joe is never objective, is always filtering and re-presenting the truth. The passage describing his wait for Clarissa at the airport illustrates this well.

Forty minutes later I was scanning the screens for arrival information. The Boston flight had only just landed and I guessed I had a half-hour wait. If one ever wanted proof of Darwin's contention that the many expressions of emotion in humans are universal, genetically inscribed, then a few minutes by the arrivals gate in Heathrow's Terminal Four should suffice. I saw the same joy, the same uncontrollable smile, in the faces of a Nigerian earth mama, a thin-lipped Scottish granny and a pale, correct Japanese businessman as they wheeled their trolleys in and recognised a figure in the expectant crowd. Observing human variety can give pleasure, but so too can human sameness. I kept hearing the same sighing sound on a downward note, often breathed through a name as two people pressed forward to go into their embrace. Was it a major second or a minor third, or somewhere in between? Pa-pa! Yolan-ta! Ho-bi! Nz-e! There was also a rising note, crooned into the solemn, wary faces of babies by long-absent fathers or grandparents, cajoling, beseeching an immediate return of love. Han-ah? Tom-ee! Let me in!

The variety was in the private dramas: a father and a teenage son, Turkish perhaps, stood in a long silent clinch, forgiving each other, or mourning a loss, oblivious to the baggage trolleys jamming around them; identical twins, women in their fifties, greeted each other with clear distaste, just touching hands and kissing without making contact; a small American boy, hoisted on to the shoulders of a father he did not recognise, screamed to be put down, provoking a fit of temper in his tired mother.

But mostly it was smiles and hugs, and in the thirty-five minutes I experienced more than fifty theatrical happy endings, each one with the appearance of being slightly less well acted than the one before, until I began to feel emotionally exhausted and suspected that even the children were being insincere. I was just wondering how convincing I myself could be now in greeting Clarissa when she tapped me on the shoulder, having missed me in the crowd and circled round. Immediately my detachment vanished, and I called out her name, in tune with all the rest.

I have worked with *Enduring Love* with students of all three English A levels, and with students of critical thinking. I don't need to tell those of you reading this book how to analyse it as English teachers, but you might be interested in how critical thinking students dealt with it and then consider whether it would be useful to add that approach to your own.

The first thing for critical thinking students to do might be to establish the facts: what is indisputable (as far as we know – I can't see that there's any mileage in suggesting that Joe wasn't really at Terminal Four and that he didn't wait 35 minutes, although my philosophy colleague might well find this worth considering!) What we're looking to do is to separate those facts from Joe's interpretations and re-presentations, in the same way in which we do with conflicting accounts about, for example, reports on battles, conspiracy theories, sporting disputes and witness statements. We're looking at something which at first seems indisputable, discussing why it's worth considering the possibility that it isn't, and then extending our learning from this to the version of events which Joe gives us in the rest of the book.

Facts?

1. Joe is at Heathrow's Terminal Four.
2. He is waiting for the Boston flight.
3. Clarissa is on this flight.
4. He waited 35 minutes.
5. He saw a wide range of people.
6. He saw a wide range of interactions.
7. He saw a man who looked Japanese.
8. He saw a woman who looked Nigerian.
9. He saw a woman with thin lips.
10. He saw a pair of female identical twins.
11. He heard a range of names being called.
12. He saw two men embracing silently.
13. He saw a small boy on the shoulders of a man, and the boy was screaming.
14. He saw the woman with them appearing angry.
15. Clarissa tapped him on the shoulder.
16. He called out her name.

What is the rest then? It's Joe's interpretation of what he sees, presented as if fact. The woman described as "a Nigerian earth mama" *may* be from Nigeria; "earth mama" is definitely subjective. A "thin-lipped Scottish granny" is not verifiable, as Joe doesn't tell us that he heard her speak nor that he has any evidence that she is a "granny". And if she had been English, would he have use a different term, such as "grandmother" or "grandma"? The man who appeared to be Japanese may have been born and brought up anywhere, and who is to say that he's a businessman? How does Joe know that he's seeing "long-absent fathers"? How does he know that the screaming boy is the son of the man who hoisted him onto his shoulders? And so on. None of these is a verifiable fact.

Critical thinking students would use their credibility criteria and ask whether Joe has any motive not to tell the truth, and here we have a key question regarding his character and his whole narrative. He does have a motive: he wants to see himself as different, as the one who is analytical, objective, uninvolved, and, therefore, an authority on the truth. He even refers to his own "detachment", which doesn't disappear until Clarissa arrives. But the air of detachment, of observing and classifying different examples of his species, is deeply ironic, as what he's doing is entirely *subjective*, attributing to people stories and relationships and histories which suit him. Now, that's not a problem here; we can just enjoy his colourful speculations and fleshing out of stories, but doesn't it make us ask ourselves about his version of other events, of other people? When he relates the whole story of himself and Jed Parry, should we believe him? Because there we do have conflicting claims: Jed's version of events and Joe's, and we can apply the "MC RAVEN" set of criteria to passages which highlight those conflicts.

- **M**otive (which might be to tell the truth, as well as to lie). We must be careful, though, not to assume that having such a motive necessarily prompts a particular response.

- **C**orroboration / **C**onflict (comparing the evidence of different witnesses, or the claims made in different documents). Again, we must be careful: we might have one uncorroborated claim but which, when the other criteria are applied, could be more credible than several that are corroborated.

- **R**eputation (of witness or of another source of evidence, such as a report).

- **A**bility to see, hear (or to know). Strictly speaking, this should be "perception", but it doesn't help our mnemonic! What we mean here is that an eye-witness account seems likely to be more credible than an account from someone who wasn't there, but we only have to think about the eye-witnesses at football matches to be reminded that even first-hand observations need to be evaluated!

- **V**ested interest. Here we have a particular motive for lying or telling the truth: the outcome is likely to benefit the source. Having a vested interest

54

might also encourage selectivity of evidence.

- Expertise (which must be relevant expertise).

- Neutrality / bias (but students need to realise that bias in itself isn't a bad thing, as long as it isn't masquerading as neutrality).

McEwan encourages us to interrogate Joe's words, to read with doubt and scepticism, through his very convincing fictitious appendix about de Clérambault's Syndrome. Here we realise that not only did we have an unreliable narrator in Joe; we had one in McEwan. The only clue he gives us in working this out is that the names of the two psychiatrists, Wenn and Camia, provide an anagram of Ian McEwan. After the "report" comes Jed's letter, presumably unmediated by Joe: is McEwan offering us this as a light on the reliability of Joe as a narrator? Or is he, by placing it next to the fictitious research, reminding us that not at any point can anything be taken as true in this story?

Jeanette Winterson plays with her readers in *Oranges are Not the Only Fruit*, even almost-but-not-quite anagrammatising her own name in Winnet Stonejar. In the same way, our first person narrator is both Winterson and not Winterson, this being both an autobiography and not an autobiography, as she indicates in her introduction. The first person narrator seems to have complete control over her material and her readers, to the extent that we wonder whether any other character is anything other than a construct of the narrator; and we have no opportunity to find out. Hers is the only version of events we have. The only version of her mother is hers. The narrative voice is that of an arch and knowing adult with a strong sense of self-protective irony, ensuring that we are kept at a distance. But just like Joe in *Enduring Love*, Jeanette inadvertently (or not?) exposes weaknesses in her narrative reliability. For example, every time the plot throws her into a situation which she can't control she escapes into fabulation, although these beautifully told stories do have their own internal logic and consistency. In using *Enduring Love* as a core text we can interrogate the credibility of the narrator in *Oranges* and, again, try to separate the facts from the possible fictions (not the fabulations and fairy tales, which don't purport to be factual). We are encouraged to ask, "What did really happen?" "What was Jeanette really like at school?" A big difference between Joe and Jeanette is that she acknowledges that, "Everyone who tells a story tells it differently, just to remind us that everybody sees it differently."

Time is a great deadener. People forget, get bored, grow old, go away. There was a time in England when everyone was much concerned with building wooden boats and sailing off against the Turk. When that stopped being interesting, what peasants there were left limped back to the land, and what nobles there were left plotted against each other.

Of course that is not the whole story, but that is the way with stories; we make them what we will. It's a way of explaining the universe while leaving the universe unexplained, it's a way of keeping it all alive, not boxing it into time. Everyone who has a story tells it differently. Some people say there are true things to be found, some people say all kinds of things can be proved. I don't believe them. The only thing for certain is how complicated it all is, like string full of knots. It's all there but hard to find the beginning and impossible to fathom the end. The best you can do is admire the cat's cradle, and maybe knot it up a bit more. History should be a hammock for swinging and a game for playing, the way cats play. Claw it, chew it, rearrange it and at bedtime it's still a ball of string full of knots. Nobody should mind. Some people make a lot of money out of it. Publishers do well, children, when bright, can come top. It's an all-purpose rainy day pursuit, this reducing of stories called history.

People like to separate storytelling which is not fact from history which is fact. They do this so that they know what to believe and what not to believe. This is very curious ...

And when I look at a history book and think of the imaginative effort it has taken to squeeze this oozing world between two boards and typeset, I am astonished. Perhaps the event has an unassailable truth. God saw it. God knows. But I am not God. And so when someone tells me what they heard or saw, I believe them, and I believe their friend who also saw, but not in the same way ...

This passage provides very fruitful material for discussion about truth, facts, history and evidence; along with all the passages quoted in this chapter it crosses over energetically from English to critical thinking and back again. To have students of both subjects work on these extracts together is a revealing experience. At the college where I work few critical thinking students choose English literature, and vice versa, (although this may not be typical) and thus they are invited to apply unfamiliar paradigms and different epistemologies to the reading of the texts and to debate their implications from different points of view. Crucially, though, they see where those points of view converge and where they can learn from each other.

Julian Barnes, in *A History of the World in 10½ Chapters* foregrounds the idea that we can place no reliance on a single version of events. He acknowledges, in the title of his "novel" that this is just *one* version of the world's history, whereas "Reader, I married him", for example, states very strongly that this is *the* history of Jane Eyre, although Terry Eagleton would not have us accept her version of events: in reviewing *How Fiction Works*, by James Wood, he writes, "The only blemish on this excellent account of author-character relations is Wood's assumption that Jane Eyre is a reliable first-person narrator, whereas in fact she is – like all of Charlotte Brontë's protagonists – malicious, self-serving and partisan." (*Prospect*, March 2008, pp 77–78)

Charlotte Brontë does anticipate postmodernism in *Villette*, when she leaves open the possibility of alternative endings to her story:
(Spoiler alert: if you haven't yet read *Villette* don't read this extract! Although the ending is ambiguous, there is information in it which will deprive you of its gradual discovery earlier in the book.)

And now the three years are past: M Emmanuel's return is fixed. It is Autumn; he is to be with me ere the mists of November come …
The sun passes the equinox; the days shorten, the leaves grow sere; but – he is coming.

Frosts appear at night; November has sent his fogs to advance; the wind takes its autumn moan; but – he is coming.

The skies hang full and dark – a rack sails from the west; the clouds cast themselves into strange forms – arches and broad radiations; … I know some signs of the sky … God, watch that sail! Oh! guard it!

The wind shifts to the west. Peace, peace, Banshee – "keening" at every window! It will rise – it will swell – it shrieks out long …

That storm roared frenzied for seven days. It did not cease till the Atlantic was strewn with wrecks …
Here pause: pause at once. There is enough said. Trouble no quiet, kind

heart; leave sunny imaginations hope. Let it be theirs to conceive the delight of joy born again fresh out of great terror, the rapture of rescue from peril, the wondrous reprieve from dread, the fruition of return. Let them picture union and a happy succeeding life.

Madame Beck prospered all the days of her life; so did Père Silas; Madame Walravens fulfilled her ninetieth year before she died. Farewell.

The first "chapter" of Barnes' book purports to tell us about Noah's Ark. So, already we have a question about reliability and logic, because we are being told about something which many people hold to be true … but this version is clearly by a different narrator. How can we judge the credibility of this narrator when (until the end of the account) we know nothing about them? What if their story conflicts with the one in the Old Testament? If we are to judge their likely credibility we need to know what their credentials are. How do we begin to piece an identity together? Well, the narrator claims to have been there; if we accept this claim we would assume that whoever it is has the ability to see. But when we realise, or rather infer, that we've just been told a story by a woodworm we say: hang on, a woodworm can't tell us a story, let alone write one … what's going on here? How did we draw the inference? We are told by the narrator that his/her/its "species" were not welcome on board the ark: they were stowaways. And then, that despite his 600 years, Noah unwisely built the entire vessel from gopher wood. "Anyone who knows anything about wood – and I speak with some authority in the matter – could have told him that a couple of dozen other tree-types would have done as well, if not better …" However, it's not until the final sentence of the story that the narrator actually reveals the species' identity. Can we apply our credibility criteria to a woodworm?

We "know" this story can't be *true* but in a strangely different way from knowing that *Jane Eyre* could be, that *Wuthering Heights* could be, that *Great Expectations* could be … or at least that they could be accepted as representations of truths; but this, surely, is just fantasy fiction, made up stuff. Ah, but, then, so are *Jane Eyre* and *Wuthering Heights*, aren't they? What are the differences? Why do we read the way we do? What expectations do we have of our writers and their stories?

That first chapter tells us that the voyage was not "some Mediterranean cruise on which we played languorous roulette and everyone dressed for dinner" and also that, "It wasn't like the nursery versions in painted wood which you might have played with as a child". Conflating time to make it obvious that this is made up? No, this is true! OK, let's go with it; let's temporarily accept the integrity and reliability of the narrator. Why? Because in first person narrative that's all we've got. We learn a lot about life on the ark, but "I realize that accounts differ. Your species has its much repeated version ..." This is the first clue we get that this narrator is unusual: "Your species". Who, or what, is it? Clues begin to emerge: "I was never chosen. In fact ... I was specifically not chosen. I was a stowaway ..."

> *When I recall the voyage, I feel no sense of obligation; gratitude puts no smear of Vaseline on the lens. My account you can trust.*

Oh yea? Says who?

Our narrator, however, continues to appear very plausible. The "ark" was in fact a flotilla of ships. (How else could the entire animal kingdom have been represented?) The 40 days and nights are also explained: more like a year and a day "by my reckoning". Now, this narrator is challenging the omniscient narrator of the original: which voice should we trust? What are we doing here? We're weighing up the version of events of a non-human stowaway on the ark against the version of events of the Bible. What is Barnes saying here?

The narrator then rolls up its/ his/her sleeves (I can't believe I'm even now wondering whether woodworm are hermaphrodite, never mind whether they have sleeves to roll up), accedes to the need for "truth", and tells us all about the vessels which comprised the "ark" and of the lives led on them. All the ships, our narrator knew about. All the goings-on too. This gets more omniscient with every sentence! And our omniscient narrator does, eventually, reveal him/herself:

> *... we were euphoric when we got off the ark. Apart from anything else, we'd eaten enough gopher wood to last a lifetime. That's another reason for wishing Noah had been less bigoted in his design of the fleet: it would have given us a change of diet ...*

And what does Barnes tell us later in the book of other events from what we call history?

> *History isn't what happened. History is just what historians tell us. There was a pattern, a plan, a movement, expansion, the march of democracy; it is a tapestry, a flow of events, a complex narrative, connected, explicable. One good story leads to another. First it was kings and archbishops with some offstage divine tinkering, then it was the march of ideas and the movement of masses, then little local events which mean something bigger, but all the time its connections, progress, meaning, this led to this, this happened because of this. And we, the readers of history, the sufferers from history, we scan the pattern for hopeful conclusions, for the way ahead. And we cling to history as a series of salon pictures, conversation pieces whose participants we can easily reimagine back into life, when all the time it's more like a multi-media collage, with paint applied by a decorator's roller rather than camel-hair brush ...*

> *We all know objective truth is not obtainable, that when some event occurs we shall have a multiplicity of subjective truths which we assess and then fabulate into history, into some God-eyed version of what 'really' happened. This God-eyed version is a fake – a charming, impossible fake ... But while we know this, we must still believe that objective truth is obtainable; or we must believe that it is 99% obtainable; or if we can't believe this then we must believe that 43% objective truth is better than 41%. We must do so, because if we don't, we're lost, we fall into beguiling relativity, we value one liar's version as much as another liar's.*

The views on history expressed in the extracts from *Oranges are Not the Only Fruit* and *A History of the World in 10½ Chapters*, whether they are those of the writers or of adopted personae, present a way of looking at things which at first seems to be the opposite of the critical thinker's way. Critical thinking has a reputation for an almost mathematical precision; all elements of an argument can be identified and named; patterns are discerned and relationships are demonstrated. The passages used for analysis in critical thinking are regarded as context free, almost. Although in the pre-2008 Credibility of Evidence paper there was a question asking students how *the context* of whatever was the focus of the dispute – war reporting, for example – might affect credibility, the remainder of the paper asked them to scrutinise, analyse and evaluate the individual claims and arguments, and to refer to nothing beyond the given texts; thence to weigh and attribute value to evidence and come to a conclusion. Thus many of my students, after working through the paper on the moon landings, argued for a conclusion which they did not believe: that it was more likely than not that the Americans didn't land on the moon. But that makes a point in itself: it was clearly counter-intuitive and it exposed the danger of selectivity of evidence and also the danger inherent in critical thinking, because it may be valid, but is it right? (Or, as we would say in critical thinking, is it sound?) However, despite the subject's "reputation" for precision, critical thinkers aren't only analysers and namers of parts: they are interpreters and evaluators. We can't always pin down causal relationships, indeed there may be circumstances in which it would be fallacious to do so. We can't always agree about things – lessons would be a lot less interesting if we did – and the more I teach critical thinking the less unlike teaching English it becomes.

That said, in the first year of my AS teaching there was only one student who took both subjects. He chose Mark Haddon's *The Curious Incident of the Dog in the Night-time* and D.C. Pierre's *Vernon God Little* for his comparative coursework. Interestingly, each has an unreliable narrator, and it was the narrative voice which the coursework concentrated on. The unreliability of Christopher, in Haddon's book, is absolutely not to do with duplicity of which he seems incapable, although yes, we only have his word for this. Christopher is a 15-year-old with Asperger's syndrome, who lives in a very different version of reality from most people, and who tells his story as disingenuously as Winterson's narrator uses disguise, subterfuge and guile. As well as being a gem of a book, it has much to interest critical thinkers.

Christopher needs logic, and is disturbed by ambiguity, inconsistency and the non-literal. He is an unsophisticated and candid narrator, in alternate chapters narrating events and presenting ideas. For example, in chapter 197 (which comes immediately after chapter 193 and before 199) he tells us:

> When I used to play with my train set I made a train timetable because I liked timetables. And I like timetables because I like to know when everything is going to happen. And this was my timetable when I lived at home with Father and I thought that Mother was dead from a heart attack (this was the timetable for a Monday and also it is an approximation).

We have no reason to doubt the veracity of any of this. Haddon has created the character so well that we believe it's just what Christopher would do. But when Christopher is out in the world – our world – we see his version of events as significantly different from our own. In chapter 197 he is on a train. That's all. It's a straightforward train journey. But it isn't straightforward for him, and because Christopher isn't good at empathising, the way he feels about the train journey – the way it is for him – becomes the reality; when he relates it he is, accordingly, telling the truth. It's not that he's saying, "Well, I know that being on a train is a pretty unremarkable experience for the majority of people but I find it very disturbing." No, he can't accommodate the first reality. He doesn't apologise for not conforming. He explains that he is unhappy, and tries to show us why. We are then able to draw the inference which concludes his argument: that we should accept his behaviour. He appears to be creating an enclosed valid argument which exists completely without reference to the real world: valid but not sound. According to his logic, he has a reason to be frightened:

> *There were lots of people on the train, and I didn't like that, because I don't like lots of people I don't know and I hate it even more if I am stuck in a room with lots of people in a room I don't know, and a train is like a room and you can't get out of it when its moving.*

What Christopher wants us to understand is that he's very uncomfortable, indeed very anxious, on the train. We need an explanation for this; is the one he gives us in the form of a valid argument? Given Christopher's security in patterns, regularity and the predictable we might expect that he would be drawn to this structure and thereby feel safe.

If we take his main point as being that he's very uncomfortable on trains, then he's simply *explaining* it by what he says; he's telling us how and why he's uncomfortable. If, however, we draw a conclusion – for example, that we should understand his apparently strange behaviour, or that the *world* should understand his apparently strange behaviour, then we have a conclusion which he wants us to accept, which would involve us changing our minds, acceding to his logic.

C: You should accept my behaviour on the train (rather than condemning it or ridiculing it) because:

R1: It is a bad thing for me to be with lots of people I don't know.

R2: It is even worse if we are all in one room together.

R3: (by analogy) A train is like a room in one respect (so what's true of a room will be true of a train).

R4: A train is not like a room in another respect: but where it's not like a room in another respect is that you can't get out of it because it's moving.

(R5: unstated, And that's worse.)

If we accept the reasons then we must, surely, draw the conclusion, shouldn't we?

Looking at it this way we are closer to Christopher's way of thinking which is based on valid and indeed sound argument. Inside his own head, his own world, the only thing that makes sense is logic. Had he claimed that being with lots of people is a bad thing (for anyone) and that being in one room together is even worse (for anyone) we would have challenged the soundness of the argument. We would insist that he support such apparent over-generalisations. But Christopher avoids this flaw, making no such universal claims and so we accept his argument.

As such, this doesn't make Christopher unreliable, in that he is at least consistent, but it does mean that we have to adjust to him, rather than wondering why he doesn't adjust to us – "us" being the people on the train, the readers, the "normal" people who aren't distressed by being in an enclosed moving space with our fellow human beings. Although once you start to think about it …

Things worsen for Christopher when the policeman reaches out to touch him, and he starts to scream. The train moves fast and his head is overwhelmed by the multiplicity of things and people in the world, and he focuses instead on doing some quadratic equations in his head.

Haddon deftly takes us into that head and once we are there everything that Christopher sees and feels seems sensible. It is we, we are made to realise, who have become unreliable narrators of our own world, glossing over the complexities and complications and not knitting our brows in perplexedness at the bizarre things we do. Christopher is the child who keeps asking us

"Why?" "Why do you do this? Why do you have that? Why does this happen?" He makes us look through his eyes at our world, and we are made to realise that it is, indeed, bizarre.

5
Waiting for Godot

If *Waiting for Godot* is, famously, a play in which "Nothing happens – twice" it may seem a strange place to look for anything to which a critical thinking approach might apply, let alone provide an enriched reading for. But the two main characters, Vladimir and Estragon, are in a hopeless situation to which they react *very differently*, and it is in exploring those differences that a critical thinking approach might add a new dimension. Indeed, it wasn't until I re-read the play with my critical thinking hat on that I really saw how different were the two characters' reactions to the situation they were in. Of course, the play will be read and studied as an existential exposure of humanity's place in "the void"; it will be explored within the genre of the absurd; be studied as tragedy, comedy and tragicomedy. But it can also be approached as a play in which one character has a rational and the other an irrational approach to their situation. The question for the audience is: which is which? This may seem obvious at the outset, but how might we feel by the end?

Estragon is the child, the one who feels and doesn't reason; Vladimir, however, keeps going by trying to locate himself in a world which can be explained and where things can be predicted. Estragon feels hunger; Vladimir finds food. Estragon suggests they hang themselves to pass the time; Estragon dreams; Estragon contemplates the moon, and describes it as "Pale for weariness … Of climbing heaven and gazing on the likes of us." Estragon is, I suggest, an extreme version of a literature student, privileging personal response over analysis, yet every now and again producing an arresting insight and surprising facility for metaphor. His classmate Vladimir, however, wants a timetable based on – well, probably critical thinking and nothing else, unless perhaps a little maths. Maybe more classes of formal logic would please him too: if he feels he isn't getting enough in critical thinking he can ask the philosophy teacher if he can have some extra tuition. Estragon can't reason, Vladimir can do little else. But which, Beckett might be saying, is the right approach? Neither? They're both equally pathetic? Or, Estragon's is the only way to respond, but not if you want to stay alive?

The play opens with Estragon saying, "Nothing to be done." So, that's him. Our introduction to Vladimir is, "All my life I've tried to put it from me, saying, Vladimir, be reasonable ..."

The two characters appear to pin their hopes of the finiteness of their uncertainties on the eventual arrival of Godot, which will make all the waiting purposeful. In fact, it's clear that this is Vladimir's construct, not Estragon's, as shown in the refrain,

Estragon   *Let's go.*

Vladimir   *We can't.*

Estragon   *Why not?*

Vladimir   *We're waiting for Godot.*

While waiting, Vladimir attempts to fill the space with critical reasoning:

Vladimir   *Do you remember the Gospels?*

Estragon   *I remember the maps of the Holy Land. Coloured they were. Very pretty. The Dead Sea was a pale blue. The very look of it made me thirsty ...*

Vladimir   *You should have been a poet.*

Estragon   *I was.* [Gesture towards his rags.] *Isn't that obvious?*

Vladimir   *The two thieves. Do you remember the story?*

Vladimir then attempts an interrogation of the Gospels, concerned with the credibility of what appear to be conflicting accounts:

Vladimir   *… how is it that of the four Evangelists only one speaks of a thief being saved.*

…

Estragon   *Well? They don't agree, and that's all there is to it.* (This student needs a critical thinking course!)

Vladimir   *But all four were there. And only one speaks of a thief being saved. Why believe him rather than the others?*

Vladimir has chosen a credibility criterion – corroboration / conflict, and might, if taught well, go on to apply others: motive, vested interest, bias, expertise, ability to see, reputation ... but the potential of this is shut down by Estragon: "People are bloody ignorant apes". Mmm – young Estragon needs a little help. Even, Gogo, if all people *are* ignorant (irrespective of whether apes are or not), does it explain why such an extraordinary turn of events is only referred to in one Gospel and remains uncorroborated, and why it would be *that* one which the "bloody ignorant apes" accept, perhaps taking the absence of the story from the others not as suggesting that it didn't happen but that for some reason it was not reported. Were the writers like a script team round a table? "OK Luke – you do that bit … After all, if we make them all the same what's the point of having four of us?" Vladimir doesn't go into the fact that this is the only instance of deviation, but then he hasn't got the best sparring partner to stimulate his thinking. Socratic dialogue doesn't get very far with Estragon around.

It's after this failed attempt at reasoning that Estragon introduces the refrain of the child, weary of the interminable car journey, usually expressed as, "Are we there yet?" His mantra is, "Let's go." In our literature class we will be pondering the meaning of this: "go" as in leave the scene (why? to go where? what for?) or "go" as in leave life (with the same associated questions). But of course, Vladimir reminds him that they can't, (do either?) because they're waiting for Godot.

They wait by a tree. Vladimir thinks it's a willow. Estragon asks, "Where are the leaves?" to which Vladimir replies fairly reasonably, "It must be dead." To which Estragon responds with the stunningly simple, direct and lyrical,

"No more weeping." Life = weeping. Death = an end to it.

Vlad the Reasoner won't give up. Ever. When Estragon asks him what they did "yesterday", Vladimir responds angrily: "Why ... nothing is certain when you're about." He *needs* certainty. He needs things to follow patterns, to make sense. He manages, for brief moments, to impose a matrix of reason, and of logic, onto the "void" which is Estragon's version of the world.

Estragon comes up with an idea for passing the time – perhaps the ancestor of Baldrick's "cunning plans":

Vladimir   *... but while waiting.*

Estragon   *What about hanging ourselves?*

Mmm – slightly flawed thinking there, although he does manage to explain to Vladimir that with only one bough at their disposal they'd need to know which of them was the heavier so that he could go second and not break the bough: "If it hangs you it'll hang anything." Estragon is good at common sense, practical stuff; he can deal with the things in front of him very effectively. He doesn't spend time trying to understand the meaning of life – because he knows there isn't any. Vladimir can't yet face this.

Later in the play Beckett introduces us to another pair of characters (although again, in another reading, we would be examining to what extent any of the four can be described as such). Pozzo, who is bombastic, assured, authoritative, possessed of the trappings of the material world, arrives with another man, Lucky, who is lead by a rope like an animal. He offers, for entertainment, to have Lucky "dance, or sing, or recite, or think". Vladimir responds to the last word with interest: "He thinks?"

Pozzo   *Certainly. Aloud. He even used to think very prettily once. I could listen to him for hours ... Would you like him to think something for us?*

Estragon doesn't really see the entertainment value here, and says that he'd rather Lucky danced because "it'd be more fun". Their preferences are in character. Estragon suggests that perhaps he could dance first and think afterwards, to which Pozzo replies "By all means, nothing simpler. It's the natural order." Perhaps Beckett could see a future filled with ill-advised and embarrassingly recorded dance-floor displays which a little forethought would have averted!

What follows, after the tortured "dancing", is a 705-word speech of unpunctuated and, at first sight, nonsensical rambling, albeit beginning with the vestiges of rational argument, starting with: "Given the existence …".

Try this passage with critical thinking and literature students, inviting them to derive a structure: to work out what's parenthetical, what's illustrative and what the argument is. You might end up with something like: "Given the existence of a personal God, it is established beyond all doubt that man is seen to waste and pine and shrink and dwindle." However, some students might end up with something quite different: good – now the different versions can be the focus for discussion, in pairs and small groups, then widening to the whole class. A visualiser and an electronic whiteboard are useful here, as the passage can be annotated and colour coded, effectively "marked up" as the discussion progresses.

The closer this analysis is, the closer students are to the text, to the meaning, and to the skill of Beckett. And what they'll do on the way is realise that *11 times* Lucky says "for reasons unknown". And they'll be able to group and categorise many of Lucky's parenthetical statements to see before them a highly distorted, but nevertheless highly recognisable version of our own existence and the things we do to try and give it meaning.

And it all seems too silly, all that stuff, if the end is that we "waste and pine", "shrink and dwindle", and we don't even know why. But Lucky, like Vladimir, clings on to the hope offered by reason: he doesn't say it's all unreasonable, doesn't say, "For no reason" but, "For reasons unknown" – thus far, unknowable, but they are *there*, whether we know them or not.

From no doubt varying motives, the others, in anguished desperation, wrestle Lucky to the end of his discourse. What might be the reasons for each of the characters being desperate for Lucky to stop? Sheer boredom, in Estragon's case? Sheer terror in Vladimir's? Sheer bullying in Pozzo's, as he uses his power over Lucky to convince himself that he is important, in control?

Early in Act Two Vladimir is questioning Estragon about his being beaten. Why, he asks Estragon, does he always come back (to Vladimir)? Estragon says that he doesn't know – again, consistent with his character. He doesn't know why he does it, but he is compelled to do it. Vladimir claims that he, however, does know; this is consistent with his need to understand what's going on in his life. Estragon comes back because he can't defend himself: Vladimir wouldn't let "them" beat him.

But Estragon claims that Vladimir couldn't have stopped them, because there were ten of them. Ah, but this isn't Vladimir's point: "No, I mean before they beat you. I would have stopped you from doing whatever it is you were doing." "I wasn't doing anything," replies Estragon. "Then why did they beat you?" asks Vladimir, looking, as ever, for an explanation. Estragon doesn't know, of course; he still believes he wasn't doing anything. "Perhaps you weren't. But it's the way of doing it that counts. The way of doing it, if you want to go on living."

The way of not doing anything – of doing nothing – is what this play is showing us. We are reminded of the first line: "Nothing to be done." Nothing is something that is to be done. And while doing it, what Vladimir is doing is no more than many of us do when faced with injustice, unfairness or tragedy: we ask why.

Vladimir is desperate to localise the void, to have a temporal and spatial existence which he can identify. "Do you not recognize the place?" he asks Estragon, unwittingly unleashing the anguished reply: "Recognize! What is there to recognize? All my lousy life I've crawled about in the mud! And you talk to me about scenery! … You and your landscapes! Tell me about the worms!"

Estragon isn't disconcerted by the fact that the tree, bare the previous day, is now covered in leaves. He is free-floating in the space-time continuum, existing nowhere and anywhere. Vladimir doesn't share his insouciance. "In a single night?" he asks incredulously. "It must be spring," is Estragon's confident reply. "But in a single night!" It just isn't making sense!

Estragon actually comes up with a good explanation – that it's not the same tree. This is clear, – well, obvious, really. But to admit to that Vladimir would have to admit to not being sure of where they are and how it relates to where they were. He spots a pair of boots: ah, here's some evidence to support his claim that it's the same tree. They must be in the same place, because Estragon left the boots there the day before. However, Estragon insists that they aren't his boots, they're a different colour. Now we have two reasons for Vladimir to accept that he isn't where he thought he was. But no, he can't do this, so he comes up with the implausible claim that someone came and took Estragon's and left his own.

"Why?" asks Estragon, and so do we. "His were too tight for him, so he took yours." So, the universe tilts back into place, pivoted by Vladimir's blinkered thinking which hides the truth. Even when the biggest flaw in the argument is exposed he doesn't change his mind: bad reasoning is better than being cast adrift without a location. When Estragon tries on the boots they are found to be too big: the other person left his too-tight boots and took some smaller ones!

Later, Pozzo and Lucky return, the former now blind and the latter dumb. Rather than being sensitive to this distressing turn of events for the two, Vladimir seizes upon the opportunity to affirm his existence. He is moved to loquaciousness and even lyricism; ironically, his prolixity delays the very thing which will do this: helping Pozzo and Lucky get up. In his musings he admits that what they do is "to prevent our reasoning from foundering". Estragon puts it succinctly: "We are all born mad. Some remain so."

Towards the end of the play the boy who had visited in Act One returns, to tell them again that Mr Godot isn't coming, but that he'll come the next day. Estragon repeats his suggestion that they hang themselves while waiting, as it will pass the time. He doesn't seem to grasp the illogicality – that by doing so they would no longer be waiting. But then again, maybe he does!

6

Rosencrantz and Guildenstern are Dead

This play is rich in critical thinking. In homage to *Waiting for Godot* it too offers an exposé of attempts at reasoning, through the fairly poor attempts of the hapless eponymous characters to make some sense of their lives.

The opening scene provides material for a whole critical thinking lesson on probability. When we first look at argument we might start with deductive reasoning, through which we draw conclusions with certainty: in a deductively valid argument we must, if we accept the reasons, accept the conclusion. Here are two claims:

> All natural blondes have higher degrees.
> I am a natural blonde.

What is an inference which we can draw from these? If we accept the two claims, what conclusion are we being invited to draw? That I have a higher degree. There is no way that anyone could not accept this conclusion, if they have already accepted the two claims. This is deductive validity. (If the claims are also true, the argument is described as sound, as well as valid.)

But most arguments we come across are *inductive*, where we're looking at the *probability* of a conclusion:

> Most of the natural blondes I know have higher degrees.
> I am a natural blonde.
> Therefore it's probable that I have a higher degree.

The amount of probability might range from 51% to 99%. Any less, and we can't say it's probable; any more and we can say it's certain.

We all know that when a coin is tossed it is as likely to come down heads as it is tails, and that each tossing of the coin is a discrete event. In the same way we recognise the fallacy of the losing gambler who keeps on playing because he or she believes that they are due a win.

We know that each roll of the die is independent of the ones before. This is logical. But sometimes we can't help ourselves, and when something that has an equal chance of going one way or another just keeps going one way, it can unsettle us.

At the start of the play Rosencrantz and Guildenstern are tossing coins. Guildenstern's bag is nearly empty; Rosencrantz's is nearly full. Guildenstern keeps tossing coins. Rosencrantz keeps calling heads. It consistently is.

Stoppard tells us that the run of heads is "impossible": well it isn't, because it's happening. How can something be both impossible and possible? Impossible and actually occurring? Rosencrantz shows no surprise at what is happening. He either has a good grasp of the notion of probability, or perhaps hasn't even thought about it. He just feels a little awkward about taking so much money from his friend.

Guildenstern, by contrast, isn't concerned about the money, but by the run of heads. He is thinking about probability, but along the lines that most of us would think: that it's just so unlikely; that in our experience it just doesn't happen. Get your class to toss coins a hundred times and record the results: see how much, or how little, variation there is.

Guildenstern, rather like Vladimir, tries to reason his way through this. Rosencrantz, like Estragon, responds only to the immediacy of the situation. This, too, disconcerts Guildenstern. Does Rosencrantz, he asks, feel no fear? "Fear! The crack that might flood your brain with light!"

The run of heads continues. Guildenstern, thinking that he's being logical, continues to search for an "explanation" of an occurrence which, he doesn't see, is simply an accretion of a series of independent events. He wants to know *why* this is happening, just like Vladimir:

> *It must be indicative of something besides the redistribution of wealth …*
> *List of possible explanations …*
> (Ask your students to try this before they read what he comes up with.)

> *One. I'm willing it. Inside, where nothing shows, I am the essence of a man*
> *spinning double-headed coins, and betting against himself in private*
> *atonement for an unremembered past.*

Now, is this someone who is going to penetrate the mind that is Hamlet's? Complete with antic disposition?

> *Two. Time has stopped dead, and the single experience of one coin being*
> *spun once has been repeated ninety times … Three. Divine intervention …*
> *Four. A spectacular vindication of the principle that each individual coin*
> *spun individually is as likely to come down heads as tails and therefore*
> *should cause no surprise each individual time it does.*

This is a play which is full of playfulness, and it's largely an intellectual play. Stoppard creates new versions of Shakespeare's ciphers and we rather like them. They are funny. They are confused. They don't know what they're supposed to be doing, nor why. They are at the mercy of more powerful forces that care nothing for them: Shakespeare, Claudius, and Hamlet. They are a lot like us, and their attempts to shine a light on the fog that envelops them have just the same effect as when we're driving our cars: the light's very good at alerting others to what we're doing, but in terms of our own illumination it merely exacerbates the murk.

Other instances in the play where critical thinking meets literature include Guildenstern's presentation on the democratic fallacy. This is the flaw in reasoning which we see in "Ten million people can't be wrong." Well, they can. What happens in class when we ask for a show of hands in response to a closed question? "Who thinks it's X?" Don't the students look around, to see how many people have their hands up? It takes courage to hold out for Y, when all around you are going for X. The "robbery" exercise described later in this book is a nice way of getting students to worry less about having answers that are different from the majority's. Another way round this is to use mini whiteboards, where students write X or Y and hold them up for the teacher to see, without the rest of the class seeing. If you are in a school or college which has the facility for it, electronic voting is even better.

Guildenstern's example is about a man who thinks he saw a unicorn. This mystical encounter becomes, through being spread more and more thinly, "A horse with an arrow in its forehead. It must have been mistaken for a deer." Everyone says so: the man was obviously wrong. Only he wasn't.

After their encounter with the player, Rosencrantz and Guildenstern meet Queen Gertrude who wants them to "instantly … visit / My too much changed son."

They have their instructions, their purpose: to "glean what afflicts him". They have their Godot, their learning objective, their purpose. Guildenstern is able to reassure Rosencrantz (and himself) that "There's a logic at work …" .

That they fail to "glean" what "afflicts" Hamlet is less significant than the fact that they had been given the task in the first place. They were no longer floundering in the mist, or lost in the void.

And what of Hamlet? What does afflict him?

Player   *Hamlet, in love with the old man's daughter, the old man thinks.*

This is, indeed, one of the many false trails laid by Shakespeare, though plausible enough. Probably true in itself, but as an explanation of Hamlet's melancholy it's mistakenly presented as a cause when it could be a correlation, or just a coincidence. Two events have occurred. Ophelia has attempted to return Hamlet's letters to him, and perhaps appears to Hamlet as compliant in the eavesdropping by Polonius and Claudius. Hamlet is acting very strangely. And although it's probably true that Ophelia becoming less close to him has worsened his melancholy, it doesn't mean it's caused it. There may be more cars on the road than ever before. There may be more cases of asthma in children than ever before. Can we infer that the former has caused the latter? (Or, even the other way round: if children are asthmatic, might parents be more inclined to drive them to school?) If we do, might we be missing another explanation for the increase in asthma?

Later, Rosencrantz asks Guildenstern, "Do you ever think of yourself as actually *dead*, lying in a box with a lid on?"

As his musings progress, we see some kind of argument structure emerge, with the conclusion that if I'm going to stuff you in a box, you'd rather be alive than dead. Why? Because you'd have a chance, you might be rescued, and you could enjoy the fact that you're not dead. It's a nice (if rather morbid) game for a critical thinking lesson.

7
Critical Thinking and Poetry

Critical thinking can lend itself to the analysis of narrative prose fiction and to drama, where characters are facing dilemmas and constructing arguments (and where the writers are constructing arguments too), but what about poetry? This is the most allusive and elusive of genres, the one which thrives on ambiguity, the one which, if pinned down to a discrete meaning can lose life, like the collector's butterfly or, as pleasures are described in Robert Burns's 'Tam O' Shanter':

> *... like poppies spread:*
> *You seize the flow'r, its bloom is shed;*
> *Or like the snow falls in the river,*
> *A moment white – then melts forever;*
> *Or like the borealis, race*
> *That flit, ere you can point their place;*
> *Or like the rainbow's lovely form*
> *Envanishing amid the storm.*

When we reach the end of a poem by Philip Larkin, for example, we are often presented with and respond to the ineffable; there is a transcendence which we absolutely do not want to pin down as the conclusion to an argument:

> *... Sent out of sight, somewhere becoming rain.*

'The Whitsun Weddings'

> *... Here is unfenced existence:*
> *Facing the sun, untalkative, out of reach.*

'Here'

77

…the deep blue air, that shows
Nothing, and is nowhere, and is endless.

'High Windows'

But there *is* a sense in which poems are arguments: the author wishes us to accept something, or be persuaded of something – essentially, to agree with them. Even making us see something familiar in a new way is a kind of argument: you thought you knew this thing; well here it is again: see it now, now that I have illuminated it for you. The poet is trying to persuade us of something of which we were not hitherto persuaded. Some poems, however, lend themselves much more easily to argument analysis than the three above, and it seems sensible to start with those. (Although we will, however, return to Larkin later.)

Compare those endings above with this, from John Donne's 'A Valediction: Forbidding Mourning':

If they be two, they are two so
*   As stiffe twin compasses are two,*
Thy soule the fixt foot, makes no show
*   To move, but doth, if th'other doe.*

And though it in the centre sit,
*   Yet when the other far doth rome,*
It leanes, and hearkens after it,
*   And growes erect, as that comes home.*

Such wilt thou be to mee, who must
*   Like th'other foot, obliquely run:*
Thy firmness draws my circle just,
*   And makes me end, where I begunne.*

We know precisely what Donne means here: his meaning will be the same as ours. It would destroy the impact if we were unsure what a pair of compasses was; Larkin's "unfenced existence" is "out of reach"; the "arrow-shower" is "out of sight" and "the deep blue air … shows / Nothing, and is nowhere, and is endless" yet the images are every bit as powerful despite their nebulousness, perhaps because of it. On a visceral level we *do* know exactly what Larkin means, but that meaning may well be unique to each of us as an individual.

'The Flea', by Donne, is described by James Reeves, editor of the *Poetry Bookshelf Selected Poems* thus: "Ingenious as it is, this is as cynical and unpleasant a poem as any Donne wrote." Perhaps that was an attitude more consistent with the cultural values of 1952, but even so it seems to assume that Donne wasn't just having a bit of fun.

Marke but this flea, and marke in this,
How little that which thou deny'st me is;
It suck'd me first, and now sucks thee,
And in this flea, our two bloods mingled bee;

Thou know'st that this cannot be said
A sinne, nor shame, nor losse of maidenhead,
*   Yet this enjoyes before it wooe,*
*   And pamper'd swells with one blood made of two*
*   And this, alas, is more than wee would doe.*

Oh stay, three lives in one flea spare,
Where wee almost, yea more than maryed are.
This flea is you and I, and this
Our marriage bed, and marriage temple is;
Though parents grudge, and you, w'are met,
And cloistered in these living walls of Jet.
*   Though use make you apt to kill mee,*
*   Let not to that, selfe murder added bee,*
*   And sacrilege, three sinnes in killing three.*

Cruell and sodaine, hast thou since
Purpled thy nails, in blood of innocence?
Wherein could this flea guilty bee,
Except in that drop which it suckt from thee?
Yet thou triumph'st, and saist that thou
Find'st not thy selfe, nor mee the weaker now;
*   'Tis true, then learne how false, feares bee;*
*   Just so much honour, when thou yeeld'st to mee,*
*   Will wast, as this flea's death tooke life from thee.*

The poem starts with "Marke" and like Lucky's opening "Given …" in *Waiting for Godot*, it suggests that there may be an argument coming. What are we to "Marke"? The flea. And why? Because it provides an analogy for you and me. It has sucked my blood and it has sucked yours; our blood is already mingled. There is nothing unsound here; it's the next move that we need to examine. No sin or shame has been involved in this co-mingling; in the same way there would be no sin or shame in our blood co-mingling in another way. Ask your students what's wrong with this as an analogy. What exactly is being compared? A flea and a human couple have far more differences than similarities, and those differences are significant, but he isn't claiming otherwise; it's the two ways in which blood may be mingled that are analogous. And if having sex were just that – mingling blood – he would have a strong analogy. What, then, makes it a disanalogy? Well, sex only "mingles blood" *metaphorically*: the flea can't possibly contain any of the bodily fluid which would be mingled if she acceded to his desires. And the very fact that the flea is an external agent invalidates the analogy anyway. Is this not like saying that in vitro fertilisation is the same as having sex? Interesting discussions follow!

The poetic voice elevates the flea hyperbolically to represent something sacred, thus claiming even more power for the analogy, but the person being addressed has a quick and conclusive answer to this: she kills the flea, thus demonstrating the falseness of an analogy which claimed that it was "you and I". The voice is equally quick, though: by killing the flea, which had sucked your blood, you are not weakened. Thus, by shedding a drop of blood through giving in to me, you will not be weakened. Suddenly, though, being weakened is likened to losing honour – where did that come from? Donne is equivocating here, shifting the meaning of a word during the course of the argument. Naughty, but clever. It's worth spending some time on equivocation with literature students, perhaps as part of a wider study of meaning which would include metaphor, ambiguity and vagueness. This is a part of the critical thinking course too, as students, particularly at A2, need to be able to identify ways in which a writer's or speaker's use of language may influence the inferences which are made.

Much poetry seeks overtly to persuade – a lover that they are loved and / or should love, for example, although, "Love me for the following reasons …" must be one of the most futile of arguments: since when has love had anything to do with reason? "Love me despite these reasons not to …" might be a bit more realistic; and, "I love you for the following reasons …" perhaps the most. But even then, is this not explaining (or attempting to) rather than reasoning?

Andrew Marvell's poetic voice in 'To His Coy Mistress', is engaged in the same business as is Donne's persona in 'The Flea'. This is a simple argument, once students have found the conclusion, which is neither at the end nor the beginning:

Now therefore …
Let us sport us while we may

We'd need to decide whether this is a genuine conclusion, supported by reasoning, or a spurious one, masquerading as the end of an argument but in fact being part of an explanation, telling us what, why or how something is as it is, rather than trying to persuade us that it is. In order to make a decision we need to look at his reasoning.

Had we but world enough and time,
This coyness, Lady, were no crime
We would sit down and think which way
To walk and pass our long love's day.
Thou by the Indian Ganges' side
Shouldst rubies find: I by the tide
Of Humber would complain. I would
Love you ten years before the Flood,
And you should, if you please, refuse
Till the conversion of the Jews.
My vegetable love should grow
Vaster than empires, and more slow;
An hundred years should go to praise
Thine eyes and on thy forehead gaze:
Two hundred to adore each breast.
But thirty thousand to the rest;
An age at least to every part,
And the last age should show your heart.
For, Lady, you deserve this state,
Nor would I love at lower rate.

> But at my back I always hear
> Time's wingèd chariot hurrying near;
> And yonder all before us lie
> Deserts of vast eternity.
> Thy beauty shall no more be found,
> Nor, in thy marble vault, shall sound
> My echoing song: then worms shall try
> That long preserved virginity,
> And your quaint honour turn to dust,
> And into ashes all my lust:
> The grave's a fine and private place,
> But none, I think, do there embrace.
> Now therefore, while the youthful hue
> Sits on thy skin like morning dew,
> And while thy willing soul transpires
> At every pore with instant fires,
> Now let us sport us while we may,
> And now, like amorous birds of prey,
> Rather at once our time devour
> Than languish in his slow-chapt power.
> Let us roll all our strength and all
> Our sweetness up into one ball,
> And tear our pleasures with rough strife,
> Thorough the iron gates of life:
> Thus, though we cannot make our sun
> Stand still, yet we will make him run.

"Had we" can be read as "If we had ..." and "This coyness, Lady, were no crime" as "Then this coyness wouldn't be a crime". A critical thinking student might represent this as:

If A is true (we had lots of time) then B is true (your denying me wouldn't be a problem).
But B isn't true (we haven't got lots of time).
Therefore A isn't true (it's the case that your denying me is a problem).

An easier introduction to this kind of argument pattern is one without the negative:

If A is true, then B is true.
A is true.
So B is true.

That second one is a deductively valid argument, also known as *modus ponens* – an argument which affirms. The A is called the antecedent; B is the consequent. The above pattern affirms the antecedent.

Going back to Marvell, with

If A is true then B is true.
A isn't true.
So B isn't true.

we have an invalid argument: he is denying the antecedent in that second line.

What's wrong with that? Well, the persona is using the lack of time to persuade his "Lady" that she must give in, but he has ignored the possibility of there being other reasons for her refusal: even if they did have all that time it might not change anything; "not A" doesn't have to mean "not B". Maybe she just doesn't fancy him. The persona has created a false dilemma, limiting the options to two. That said, it has at first reading the appearance of a valid argument and surely Marvell, like Donne, is capable of writing valid arguments and is likely, therefore, to be misusing logic deliberately. Perhaps Marvell is having a go at the persona, for trying to win the woman through blinding her with (faulty) logic, and is assuming that she won't work it out. He's cheating, in order to get what he wants – but you've got to admire him for the effort!

Marvell plays with this faulty reasoning throughout the poem, giving lots of examples of how brilliant it would be if they had time and lots of examples of ways in which things would be pretty awful because they don't.

Poems have, can and should be used to persuade on matters of principle and morality. Wilfred Owen's 'Dulce et Decorum Est' tells us that if we could see, if we could hear the dying men, we would not tell children that it is sweet and honourable to die for their country. This might be read as an intermediate conclusion, leading to a further inference which Owen expects us to draw:

therefore you should not do it, or even, therefore you must not do it. Why must you not do it?

You must not do it because it is a lie. Thus,

R1:   This is a lie.
(R2:   a principle, which is assumed – lying is morally wrong.)
C: You must not do it.

What Owen needs to do, though, is to prove that it is a lie, that it is *not* sweet and honourable to die for one's country. How does he do this?

> *Bent double, like old beggars under sacks,*
> *Knock-kneed, coughing like hags, we cursed through sludge,*
> *Till on the haunting flares we turned our backs*
> *And towards our distant rest began to trudge.*
> *Men marched asleep. Many had lost their boots*
> *But limped on, blood-shod. All went lame; all blind;*
> *Drunk with fatigue; deaf even to the hoots*
> *Of tired, out-stripped Five-Nines that dropped behind.*
>
> *Gas! Gas! Quick boys! – an ecstasy of fumbling,*
> *Fitting the clumsy helmets just in time;*
> *But someone was still yelling out and stumbling*
> *And flound'ring like a man in fire or lime …*
> *Dim, through the misty panes and thick green light,*
> *As under a green sea, I saw him drowning.*
>
> *In all my dreams, before my helpless sight,*
> *He plunges at me, guttering, choking, drowning.*
>
> *If in some smothering dream you too could pace*
> *Behind the wagon that we flung him in,*
> *And watch the white eyes writhing in his face,*
> *His hanging face, like a devil's sick of sin;*
> *If you could hear, at every jolt, the blood*
> *Come gargling from the froth-corrupted lungs,*
> *Obscene as cancer, bitter as the cud*
> *Of vile, incurable sores on innocent tongues, –*

My friend, you would not tell with such high zest
To children ardent for some desperate glory,
The old Lie: Dulce et decorum est
Pro patria mori

The first stanza contains a series of descriptions of the awfulness of what is happening to the soldiers; the second a description of a gas attack; the third, the effect of the gas attack on the persona. In the fourth stanza is the implication that if it's had this effect on him it would have the same effect on you. However, you can't be here, so what is he going to do about that? Because you could say, well, I'm not there, I can't see and hear, so I'm not going to stop telling people it's honourable to die for their country.

If A (you could see and hear) then B (you'd stop).
Not A (you can't see and hear).
Therefore not B (you don't stop).

But this is our friend denying the antecedent again. What can Owen do about this? A reader could justifiably reply, well, even if I agree with you that being there would make me stop, you know that I'm not there: the thing that would make me stop isn't happening. So I won't stop.

Owen knows that we can't see or hear, but he nevertheless pursues the argument because in so doing he is trying to *make* us see and hear. He's trying to turn it into a valid argument through his use of poetic technique: his powerful imagery and the phonological features of the poem. It's vital to him that we see and hear. This is his responsibility to his comrades. This is why he uses such shocking imagery and such uncompromising description. This changes the argument structure to:

If A (you could see and hear) then B (you'd stop saying it).
A (you do see and hear, through my words).
Therefore B (you stop).

This is affirming the antecedent, a valid argument pattern. What's really important is that, in understanding the difference between the two patterns, we come to realise how crucial and how skilful is Owen's vivid depiction of the experiences of the soldiers.

Owen's 'The Parable of the Old Man and the Young' uses a different method of persuasion, in which we follow a narrative and are invited (or compelled) to infer a conclusion. Different readers may draw different conclusions:

> *So Abram rose, and clave the wood, and went,*
> *And took the fire with him, and a knife.*
> *And as they sojourned both of them together,*
> *Isaac the first-born spake and said, My Father,*
> *Behold the preparations, fire and iron,*
> *But where the lamb, for this burnt-offering?*
> *Then Abram bound the youth with belts and straps,*
> *And builded parapets and trenches there,*
> *And stretched forth the knife to slay his son.*
> *When lo! an Angel called him out of heaven,*
> *Saying, Lay not thy hand upon the lad,*
> *Neither do anything to him, thy son.*
> *Behold! Caught in a thicket by its horns,*
> *A Ram. Offer the Ram of Pride instead.*

But the old man would not so, but slew his son,
And half the seed of Europe, one by one.

What's the argument?

R1:   God commands Abram to slaughter his son.
(R2:   assumed – This is a bad thing.)
C: This is a wicked God.

Or

R1:   God commands Abram to slaughter his son.
(R2:   This is a bad thing.)
R3:   Abram, however, accepts this.
IC: Faith can overcome all else.
C?:   Faith is the most important determiner of what we do.
? Faith is extremely dangerous and destructive.

How we construct the argument about Abram is of course instrumental in our understanding of the argument about the war, for Owen describes his argument as a parable. A parable is a story, and as such more complete than an analogy, but the purpose of each is the same. Owen is arguing that an all-powerful authority commanding a trusting subject to slaughter his son is just what is happening in the war; but that in the former case God, having seen how faithful Abram was, provided an alternative sacrifice, whereas no such thing was happening in the case of the war. So here is the point at which the situation Owen is arguing about (the war) departs from the story that is key to the poem. Up to that point we could say that we're dealing with analogy, perhaps one to show that the leaders in Europe are, like God, wise and just, and are not interested in senseless slaughter for their own self aggrandisement and to affirm their power. However, given that those leaders, represented by "the old man" do not act as God did, we see that they had none of God's mercy and wisdom. Conclusion; this war is killing millions because of the pride of the leaders. It is a wicked war.

There is a connection between these two Owen poems and my next example, as we move from the battlefields of the Western Front to the back garden of 105 Newland Park, Hull. When we were confronted in 2003 with the prospect of Britain's invasion of Iraq, many students and staff at the college gathered in the theatre to share our views and feelings, focusing on peace rather than war, hope rather than despair.

I chose on that occasion in the theatre to read Larkin's 'The Mower' because its final lines said what I wanted to say in the best way possible. It was only later that I looked at the poem with a critical thinking class and we discussed whether we had an argument.

'The Mower' is available in Larkin's *Collected Poems*, published by Faber. It tells us about what happened when a hedgehog, concealed in some long grass, was accidentally run over by a lawnmower. The hedgehog had previously been fed by the person doing the mowing. This incident causes the persona to reflect on life and death.

Is there a line of reasoning in 'The Mower'? Is there a conclusion, stated – if so what is it? Or to be drawn by the reader – and if so what? As readers of poetry we are more attuned to the latter; part of the joy of engaging with a poem is that we are actively involved in the creative process, in entering into dialogue with the poet and drawing our conclusion. So it's not such an unnatural thing to open with a question about a conclusion, rather than the more usual, "what does it mean?" That is, of course, a preliminary to the key question in literary study – "*how* does it mean?"; in looking at argument structure we are actually investigating that as well. So, is there something here which the writer wants us to accept / be persuaded of / agree with? And if so, what are the reasons supporting the conclusion? In looking for conclusions we look for words like "therefore" and "so", like "should" and "must".

> *... we should be careful*
> *Of each other, we should be kind*
> *While there is still time.*

Is this a conclusion, in the critical thinking sense? Well, he's using "should", twice, which suggest that he is trying to persuade us of something: that we be kind to each other. What reasons has he given? What evidence? Are there any flaws in his argument?

The argument rests on analogy: the gardener has been careless and in one careless moment he has ended a life. In the same way, our carelessness can be responsible for the deaths (literally and metaphorically) of others. If we don't want to be responsible for the deaths (or the hurting) of others we should take more care. The other thing which emerges is that, because a life can be ended so suddenly, we should ensure that we are as kind as we can be.

Is it a strong analogy? And what else is the hedgehog incident being used as? Evidence? Well, if his whole argument rests on one incident, isn't his conclusion wildly overdrawn? How can you get to the conclusion that we should be kind to each other, from the death of a hedgehog? But you can, you do – he has! The experience (and in this case we do know that it was an experience rather than an imagined event) has made him think, and given the conflation of poetic thought it's taken him right to the big issue of human life. A critical thinking student – and a literature student – could now inflate that process, imagine his thought processes; re-create the mental journey which took him from the one incident to the conclusion. This is a fascinating exercise to observe both groups of students doing, and it has all the advantages of bringing students closer to the poem, allowing a different way of reading, helping literature students become critical thinkers and critical thinking students to read poetry.

In 'This be the verse', from *High Windows* there is no doubt about what the poetic voice is wanting to persuade us of: "Get out as early as you can, / And don't have any kids yourself."

The conclusion is in those last two lines, supported by the reason in the preceding two. Is any evidence given to support the reason? Well the first two stanzas purport to present that. But is he generalising from a single example? If so, this is faulty reasoning and the conclusion is too strong for the reasons. But perhaps the first two stanzas are, actually, based on an accretion of many examples, as implied in the pronoun "your" – a colloquial version of "one", and the implication of the plural "fools", so maybe this isn't such a bad argument after all!

If we accept "They fuck you up, your mum and dad" as a proposition, it becomes R1. R1 is expanded upon in "They fill you with the faults they had / And add some extras, just for you." So, he's explained what he means by "fucking up" and given that, we have to agree that being fucked up is not a good thing. Does the middle stanza of the poem give us any more reasons to accept the conclusion? It seems at first to be irrelevant to the argument (though not to the poem), but wait, he writes later that "man hands on misery to man" and if we accept this as a reason then the stanza preceding it can be seen as an explanation to go with it.

Our structure is now:

R1:   Your parents fucked you up (plus explanation of what this involves).
R2:   It's inevitable that you will do the same.
C: So, unless you want to continue the misery, don't have children.

The next question might be about R2: is it inevitable?

Your parents were messed up.
They messed you up too.
So you'll mess up your children (IC?).
So don't have any.

But, even if we accept the persona's view that he is "fucked up", could he be mistaking a correlation for a cause? He might be "fucked up", but might that have been caused by something other than his parents? And even if it were them, and their parents before them, we can only suggest the probability of him and us doing the same, so the strongest conclusion would be it's *probably* better not to have children. Another writer, or another of Larkin's poetic voices, might even have drawn the opposite conclusion: yes, things have been repeatedly bad, but you should stop the cycle of misery by being a better parent!

Lyrical Ballads, 1798, contains some of the most persuasive poems ever written in English. In the context in which they were written they were undoubtedly designed to make people think and to change their minds – not just about poetry, but about social justice. They do this without any apparent characteristics of argument – indeed, many are written in the unanalytical narrative voice of the unsophisticated folk whose plights Wordsworth and Coleridge are depicting. The conclusions are never there: they are all to be drawn. After reading, for example, 'The Female Vagrant', an early question can be: if we were to take this as an argument, what is the writer trying to persuade us to do or to think? "That such people as this should be helped not blamed"? "That she is only in that position because of the heartlessness of the rest of society"? "That the greed of the rich and the callousness of warmongers have left this woman in this position"? "That the dependence of women on men, whether fathers or husbands, has led to this situation"?

But an argument isn't just an assertion: it must prove something by reasoning. We need evidence and reasons, and it must be demonstrable that a conclusion follows from the evidence or reasons.

'The Female Vagrant' is, of course, a very long poem, which readers will find in the Penguin Classics edition.

The poem begins with some scene setting, in which we learn that the "vagrant" had a happy and secure life and was virtuous. We then have a description of the events which brought her to her present condition, where the reader is invited to make a connection between the enclosure of land, the greed of the landlord, the cannibalistic recruiting of a war-mongering, oppressive government and a life of destitution. We are invited to find explanations for the woman's plight, and thence to conclude that she is a victim, not a perpetrator, of crime. She doesn't ask us to do this: Wordsworth skilfully makes any other conclusion impossible to draw.

In the longest poem of the collection, 'The Rime of the Ancient Mariner', we are never given a reason why the mariner shot the albatross, and that seems to be just the point: it is for his utterly purposeless act that he must suffer, and the detailed delineation of his suffering, combined with the lines

He prayeth well who loveth well
Both man and bird and beast.

He prayeth best who loveth best,
All things both great and small

encourages us to draw a powerful conclusion: that we must not kill gratuitously. This appears also to be the underlying principle of the poem. Principles can function as reasons – or even as the only reason – or as conclusions. Sometimes they are not stated, but assumed. Principles can be very powerful reasons, but where someone doesn't have the same principles then we need to argue, with further reasons, evidence and perhaps examples, to support our conclusion. Coleridge seems to be saying that the power of the principle, which is also the conclusion, is demonstrated through his account of what happens to someone who ignores this principle. The wickedness of the act is implied in the severity of the punishment. This is interesting – is it valid? The reasoning goes like this: if you do something very bad you will receive a very severe punishment. You received a very severe punishment; therefore you must have done something bad.

If A then B.
B
Therefore A.

This affirms the consequent, and is not a valid argument pattern. What other explanations could there be, then, for what happened to him? Is the mariner wrong in his judgement that it was his wanton act of killing the albatross which brought about all his misfortune? Is he assuming a causal relationship where none exists? Is he falling prey to the *post hoc ergo propter hoc* fallacy: this happened after that, therefore it must have been caused by that. Although this may be counter to our intuitions about the poem, given our knowledge of the position which Coleridge and Wordsworth took regarding man and nature, it makes us look at the poem again. After all, it's not the voice of the poet which is saying the above lines, but the mariner, who has earlier appeared deranged, damaged; who has undergone dreadful privations and continues to do so, relieved, temporarily, only by his telling of the story. The mariner sees this as the only way in which he can expiate his dreadful guilt, the only way he can try and pay the price and perform penance for his deed; but what if he's wrong? What if he just suffered all those dreadful things **for no reason**? In addition to being an argument about man's relationship with nature, 'The Ancient Mariner' could be read as an example of the cruelty of a godless world, or even worse, the cruelty of a god. Or maybe, even, about the power of delusion. After all, we only have the mariner's version of events: there is no intervention from an omniscient narrator, and no interrogation from the listener. If we accept the story of the events which happened on the ship as being true, we must also accept that for much of the voyage the mariner was suffering from delusions. Do we accept as rational and believable, an account of delusions from someone who may still be delusional?

Coleridge has written elsewhere about the effect of the natural environment on the spirit. In 'The Dungeon', for example, he advocates an amazingly modern attitude towards "crime", promulgating the restorative powers of nature which contrast with the effect of confining an ill person to a small space with nothing to contemplate but his or her own misery: this misery can only be internalised, and grow, whereas nature

> *Healest thy wandering and distempered child:*
> *Thou pourest on him thy soft influences,*
> *Thy sunny hues, fair forms, and breathing sweets,*
> *Thy melodies of woods, and winds, and waters,*
> *Till he relent, and can no more endure*
> *To be a jarring and dissonant thing …*
> *His angry spirit healed and harmonized*
> *By the benignant touch of love and beauty.*

The sentiment behind this poem provides a good debating topic in a critical thinking lesson, centred as it is on the attitude to and consequent treatment of "each poor brother who offend against us", as well as in the current tendency to prescribe fresh air and exercise to those suffering from mild depression. (When Wordsworth wrote that his "heart leapt up" he too was way ahead of his time in recognising the restorative and energising possibilities of nature.)

Nature is most often seen in *Lyrical Ballads* as a positive influence. Exceptions do occur: in 'The Female Vagrant' and 'The Ancient Mariner', being on a lengthy sea voyage gives rise to mental and spiritual dislocation and fragmentation. Is this because the sea is a hostile arm of nature, or because in the case of the two protagonists they were bearing such dreadful spiritual burdens that they responded to the sea at times *as if* hostile? And how does this then affect our understanding of the mariner's version of events, and his reasoning that he is suffering because he shot the albatross? If nature is benign, then the sea itself could not have harmed him and thus all the terrors and torments were either from the supernatural or from his own mind, which is how the vagrant sees what happened to her.

In 'We are seven' Wordsworth turns the tables on the poetic voice – perhaps himself – as his exasperated narrator fails to convince the little girl that she's wrong in claiming that she is one of seven children – " 'Twas throwing words away".

> ... *"Sisters and brothers, little Maid,*
> *How many may you be?"*
> *"How many? Seven in all," she said*
> *And wondering looked at me.*
>
> *"And where are they? I pray you tell."*
> *She answered, "Seven are we;*
> *And two of us at Conway dwell,*
> *And two are gone to sea.*
>
> *"Two of us in the church-yard lie,*
> *My sister and my brother;*
> *And, in the church-yard cottage, I*
> *Dwell near them with my mother."*
>
> *"You say that two at Conway dwell,*
> *And two are gone to sea,*
> *Yet ye are seven! – I pray you tell,*
> *Sweet Maid, how this may be."*
>
> *Then did the little Maid reply,*
> *"Seven boys and girls are we;*

Two of us in the church-yard lie,
Beneath the church-yard tree."

"You run about, my little Maid,
Your limbs they are alive;
If two are in the church-yard laid,
Then ye are only five."

"Their graves are green, they may be seen,"
The little maid replied,
"Twelve steps or more from my mother's door,
And they are side by side.

"My stockings there I often knit,
My kerchief there I hem;
And there upon the ground I sit,
And sing a song to them."

We have a dispute: do we have an argument? There is logic in what the child says. For example, the narrator accepts that the two who are "gone to sea" count as part of the family, but not that the two who "in the church-yard lie" do. The child, however, can locate the latter two any time she wants, whereas the whereabouts of the former are unknown to her and, indeed, they may never return. They are "gone" in a way that the other two are clearly not. Furthermore, her grammar emphasises her perception of the continuing presence of the two children whom the narrator – somewhat heartlessly – insists, in the final stanza, are "dead". (He is "throwing words away", as they don't seem to have the same understanding of the word.) Grammar keeps people with us: a widower does not stop talking about "my wife"; a bereaved parent does not cease to mention "my child". When the relationship ceases to exist we say "ex-wife": implying still alive but no longer my wife. We use no such negation for a spouse who has died. The brother and sister of the little girl "lie" in the churchyard: they can be located and they are doing something, so they can't be lost.

The child will not be moved. Wordsworth privileges her words and it is the narrator, not she, who is made to look a little ridiculous. Is it an argument? The child is claiming that there are seven of them, and provides evidence to challenge the narrator's claim that they are only five. This disagreement goes no further than that, but it does hinge on the different understanding of the same words, and this is an important aspect of critical thinking. We must always clarify our definitions and ensure that, in an argument which is against another, each "author" means the same thing when using the same words. Both English and critical thinking classes have had lively and fruitful discussions about where the problem lies in 'We are seven', and the two different interpretations of the word "dead". In addition, just asking the question, "Is there an argument here?" opens up an interesting way of looking at the poem. After all, we all read it and make a judgement about which of the two views we most agree with: isn't that something like drawing a conclusion?

Many of the poems in the 1798 version of *Lyrical Ballads* may be read as argument, but as arguments where we are invited to draw a conclusion, to infer it, rather than having it stated for us. Here is a common characteristic of reasoning and poetry appreciation: for surely it is more exciting and more powerful where we derive our own meaning from the poem and where we draw our own conclusion from an argument which does not include a conclusion. There is engagement, a sense of participating in the writer's thinking, and then an encouragement, certainly in class discussion, to return to the argument or the poem in order to justify the conclusion which one has drawn. This is far from the "anything goes" prejudice which some have about studying poetry: the thing I like about literature, some will say, is that there's no right or wrong. (Whereas, they might say, in critical thinking there is always a right and wrong.) But in fact an argument in critical thinking can lead to more than one conclusion: reasons and evidence can lend themselves to many different positions. At the same time there can be wrong readings of poems in the sense that there is absolutely nothing in the poem which can be used to support the reading. One of the many great things about studying poetry is that we are, certainly, in a world where a single "answer" may not appear, but where we therefore have to be even more analytical, careful and thoughtful readers in order to ensure that our own reading is credible and draws its interpretation only from the poem. I hope that this chapter has shown how some of the approaches used in critical thinking can enhance this skill.

8

The Resolution of Dilemmas

Unit 3 of the first A level in critical thinking introduced ethical theories, and thus added a new dimension to the weighing of evidence and the resolution of dilemmas. Some understanding of and ability to apply utilitarian ethics, deontological ethics and libertarian ethics helped students to better explore and more comprehensively analyse the issues presented in the course, in other courses, and in life. Of the new A levels, AQA has as part of Unit 3, "ethical arguments", "developing a strategy for informed decision making" and "the concept of value in relation to decision making"; OCR's Resolution of Dilemmas unit "remains largely the same", in terms of content. For the teacher of English what is interesting is how the approaches to dilemmas and decision making can inform the study of a wide range of texts.

As an introduction to these approaches, I'll use the activity with which I introduced them to the students just starting A2 critical thinking, fresh from their AS exams and probably much preferring to be starting their long summer holidays. I gave them the three handouts which follow. I used the plot of *Hamlet*, but could equally have chosen many other A level English texts; I subsequently adapted the idea as an introduction to *Macbeth* for my GCSE class.

The first handout presented a scenario:

> You are the son* of a powerful man* – perhaps a king, an emperor, a business mogul, head of a Mafia family ...
>
> While you were out of the country, at university, your father died.

You might expect to inherit the throne / business, etc. but, quite legally, your uncle (your father's brother) marries your mother (newly widowed) and thus they become jointly in charge. (The rules of the game wouldn't allow her to take charge on her own, and nor could he.)

Now, you don't necessarily mind not taking over; you're much more interested in living your own life abroad. You are, of course, distraught about the loss of your father, but what really sickens you is that your mother has married your uncle, and so soon. You feel she has betrayed your father, and done so with a man who cannot in any way compare with him.

This makes you feel rotten. You might even contemplate suicide. But, being such a contemplative person, that's all you do.

Well, this is all bad enough, but then you receive what seems to be cast iron evidence that your father was murdered. And by your uncle. And you know what you are supposed to do: you're supposed to kill your uncle.

This is a bit of a problem for you. You are not a killer. Your uncle is very powerful and highly respected, the country is on the edge of war and, finally, your mother seems very happy.

What should you do?

*The culture in which you live is, alas, entirely patriarchal.

The second handout gave some guidance:

Step 1
To get to the heart of the dilemma and its possible resolution you'll need to flesh out the scenario, which has deliberately been left open. Here's an opportunity for some creativity!

Consider:

- who is involved
- where is the scenario taking place
- when
- what is the evidence that seems "cast iron"? (remember your credibility criteria from AS?)

The person with the dilemma is an academic, and probably good at reasoning: how might that affect what happens?

Step 2
All of the above might change the way the dilemma is dealt with, but can you suggest other variables which might also be significant?

Step 3
Read the handout on the continuum of choice and the criteria of choice. *
Create a continuum of choice for your character.
Decide which criteria would be relevant to apply in making a judgement about the choices on your continuum.

* We will be covering this in much more detail, of course, using *Critical Thinking for A2* by Roy van den Brink-Budgen.

As this is just an introduction to A2 the handout is by no means comprehensive, but it gives you a flavour of the way we would approach a dilemma like this.

The third handout was a very brief introduction to the continuum of choice and the criteria for judgement; just sufficient for this short summer course.

Questions of choice often appear to have only two answers, such as yes or no, I will / I won't, I do / I don't, you should / you shouldn't. However, there is often a much more subtle range than this, even with a simple example like, "Shall I go to college today?" The obvious answer is yes, but there might be a compelling reason to say no (you're feeling rotten, you've no money for the bus and it's pouring with rain, you need to stay off and finish your coursework for English. Compelling for you, anyway.) But you might also consider, "Yes, but later this morning" or "Yes, but I'll go in after lunch." What would you take into account in order to come to a decision?

Our example (the young man who is faced with the responsibility of killing his uncle) has a lot more scope, and is likely to have a much bigger range of answers. With these sorts of "What should we do about ..." questions we can have a whole lot of possibilities, some of which might not rule out the others. We can represent these choices as a continuum, moving from something at one extreme to something at the other, with any number of gradations in between. (Where you put the various choices along the line is one of your early challenges.)

OK, so that's that: we can see what we're dealing with. But how do we decide between all the possibilities? Well, we establish criteria for judging them. Criteria might include practicability, cost (to an individual, a state, an organisation), public opinion and rightness and wrongness. What are the rights and wrongs of right and wrong? We'll look at these with an introduction to ethical ideas, giving you different ways of looking at problems based on how to judge what's "right". Three of the theories we'll look at are utilitarianism, deontological theory ("duty ethics") and libertarianism. More will follow. For the purpose of this very early introductory activity we'll keep our definitions pretty simple.

Utilitarians consider the effects of actions and judge those which maximise the well-being or welfare of the most number of people to be the best. Where utilitarianism focuses on the consequences of actions, deontology says that something can be judged right or wrong without waiting to see what effect it has. The key part of the word comes from the Greek for "duty". Deontological ethics will attempt to tell us that we have certain

> moral obligations or duties, such as the duty not to kill, or to protect the innocent or weak.
>
> Libertarians are concerned with the freedom of the individual, a hot topic considering the new smoking laws were introduced in England in 2007. Libertarians might argue that people should be entitled to smoke, even though it's harmful, because what's important is having the freedom to choose.

I appended the above with a strong health warning to the effect that these are gross oversimplifications, but it was post-exam June, after all!

The critical thinking students worked hard on this over several lessons, most of them acknowledging that there was no easy solution and that it could all end in tears (although one of the two who recognised *Hamlet* chose to resolve it happily!).

That was a critical thinking exercise, based on a literary text; literary texts are full of dilemmas and people failing to resolve them, and the critical thinking approach can be applied to them by literature students.

Wuthering Heights is full of conflict and difficult decisions. For example, the younger Catherine believes that Linton Heathcliff is literally dying for lack of her (a conviction arising from her trust in the words of his father, Heathcliff, whom the reader knows could be lying), but also that visiting him would kill *her* ailing father, Edgar Linton, (this conviction arising from her faith in Nelly Dean, whom the reader is more likely to trust).

This section of the novel explores the anguish of a person who only wants to do good and who is placed in a situation where doing good for one vulnerable person can only harm another.

Edgar Linton tells his daughter, "You will know hereafter, darling, why I wish you to avoid his house and family – now, return to your old employments and amusements, and think no more about them." Catherine is forbidden to see or communicate with Linton, yet sends him notes via a "milkfetcher"; when Nelly Dean rummages in Catherine's drawer she is "surprised to discover a mass of correspondence …". At this point Cathy has tried to resolve the dilemma by deceiving her father, but of course she reckoned without the virtually omniscient Nelly Dean. When she discovers the letters are missing she begs for them back, and begs Nelly not to tell Edgar. When there are no more secret letters, Heathcliff eventually arrives at the gates of The Grange, only to be told by Catherine that she won't speak to him, because her father says he is a wicked man. Heathcliff responds with:

> '… you dropped Linton … into a Slough of Despond … As true as I live, he's dying for you – breaking his heart at your fickleness, not figuratively, but actually … he'll be under the sod before summer, unless you restore him!'
>
> …
>
> 'I swear Linton is dying … And grief and disappointment are hastening his death.'
>
> …
>
> 'He pines for kindness, as well as love; and a kind word from you would be his best medicine. Don't mind Mrs Dean's cruel cautions, but be generous, and contrive to see him. He dreams of you day and night, and cannot be persuaded that you don't hate him, since you neither write nor call.'

This turns out to be largely true, although we of course question whether Heathcliff's motive is really and only that of a loving father – but how would Catherine know otherwise, when no-one has explained to her why she shouldn't go to Wuthering Heights, and just how Heathcliff is "wicked"?

Heathcliff's words are powerfully persuasive, but are countered by this from Nelly in relation to Edgar Linton:

> 'Cathy! I'll not disguise, but you might kill him, if you were wild and reckless, and cherished a foolish, fanciful affection for the son of a person who would be glad to have him in his grave …'

Cathy responds:

> 'I'll never – never – oh, never, while I have my senses, do an act, or say a word to vex him.'

However, Edgar and Nelly fall conveniently ill for a few days, and Catherine is enticed to The Heights, without her father knowing. She tells Linton that if only she had her father's consent she would spend half her time up there with him.

Of course, Detective Nelly eventually discovers the deception, but this time Cathy appears more resolute:

> *'I can't be prevented from going to Wuthering Heights, except by inflicting misery on two people – whereas if you'll only not tell papa, my going need disturb the tranquillity of none.'*

That was good thinking! Now it's Nelly's dilemma. What should she do? What would you do? What would be the determining criteria for making your decision? For Nelly it's simple: deontologist that she is, she goes straight to Edgar, inflicting pain thereby on him, on Cathy and on young Linton.

This is a reminder of the conflict experienced by the first Catherine when, after Heathcliff's return, she cannot understand how her erstwhile gentle and loving husband cannot tolerate her closeness to Heathcliff. She is unable to resolve the conflict between them and instead takes it within herself, to mortal effect:

> *'Well, if I cannot keep Heathcliff for my friend – if Edgar will be mean and jealous, I'll try to break their hearts, by breaking my own.'*

The question was not so much, "What should she do?" but "What could she do?", given that her nature was incapable of deception (unlike that of her daughter, whose decision was to visit Linton, but keep the fact from her father).

Cathy later recalls what happened next:

> *'I remember being in the parlour … and Edgar being cruelly provoking, and me running into this room, desperate – As soon as ever I had barred the door, utter blackness overwhelmed me, and I fell on the floor – I couldn't explain to Edgar how certain I felt of having a fit, or going raging mad … I feared for my reason … I wish I were a girl again, half savage and hardy and free … I'm sure I should be myself were I once among the heather on those hills.'*

These situations give a critical thinking class good material to work with; literature students could use the critical thinking approach to really appreciate the difficulties of both characters and the skill of the writer in making these so real. Empathy is enhanced through the students getting to grips with the dilemmas and trying to work through them, using skills borrowed from critical thinking. They are likely to discover just how difficult they are to resolve.

Catherine Earnshaw / Linton and Catherine Linton / Earnshaw are torn by a selfish and unselfish love respectively. Still earlier in the novel Emily Brontë had foreshadowed the former's dilemma about how she should behave on Heathcliff's return. Heathcliff's disappearance upon discovering that Cathy was to marry Edgar hadn't resolved the dilemma, but merely postponed the need for it to be resolved. Having accepted Edgar's proposal Cathy describes herself as "very unhappy". What's wrong? What needs resolving? What's the dilemma? What should she do about reconciling the expectations of society – and herself – and the need for her self to be fulfilled in psycho-spiritual union with Heathcliff?

We could borrow from Unit 3 of A level critical thinking and create a continuum of choice to help Cathy deal with the problem of what to do about Heathcliff. At one end, on marrying Edgar she relinquishes all contact with Heathcliff; at the other she abandons Edgar. In between? She insists on Edgar allowing her to see him, or she maintains a distant contact, under Edgar's rules or she maintains contact illicitly.

Which criteria are important? Is Cathy a libertarian, insisting on behaviour which is outside society's accepted norms? She wishes to continue to do this, putting libertarian principles before deontological ones, but what has she failed to consider? What about Heathcliff? What about Edgar? An interesting point emerged from a lesson on this, where it was suggested that we apply utilitarian ethics. At first glance it seems obvious that Cathy seeing Heathcliff illicitly would weigh the well-being of two people (Cathy and Heathcliff) against that of one (or even of none, as Edgar wouldn't know). But no, some students said, because Cathy could not be happy in deceiving Edgar. And then again, maybe Heathcliff would be happier if Edgar knew, because that would make *him* the most unhappy. We debated whether this would be the case, or whether Heathcliff would in fact be happier in the deceit, as this would bestow power and control: he would know something that Edgar didn't; he would be the only one who knew everything about Cathy. Would Cathy be able to accommodate these different motivations of Heathcliff?

Why, Nelly wants to know, does she love Edgar? Because:

- he is handsome;
- he is pleasant to be with;
- he is young and cheerful;
- he loves me;
- he will be rich;
- I shall be the greatest woman in the neighbourhood.

And yet she is still unhappy.

> *'In whichever place the soul lives – in my soul, and in my heart, I'm convinced I'm wrong.'*

The criteria for marrying Edgar suggest that it is the right thing to do. But being "right" makes her unhappy, and to her that means it's wrong.

Whatever Cathy chooses she will have to lose something, and it's a matter of what she can lose while retaining her life, her life force and her reason for living. Ask students to identify the dilemma, construct the continuum, and apply the criteria. Can they come to a resolution? Or only a compromise? What's the difference?

Hamlet contains more than the most famously expressed dilemma in English Literature: "To be, or not to be?". The Prince of Denmark also has to decide what to do about what the ghost of his father has told him, and the horns of the dilemma are kill Claudius or let him live. Although literature students would be working with the whole play, critical thinkers can be introduced to the first few scenes, to establish that King Hamlet is dead, his brother has gained the throne and the widow; Claudius is statesmanlike and apparently assured in his public presence; the ghost of Hamlet's father tells him that Claudius murdered him and that he, young Hamlet, must take his revenge.

Hamlet has to construct a continuum of choice. Asking English students to do this we might have:

- kill Claudius;
- get someone else to do it;
- let Claudius know he knows;
- let Gertrude know he knows;
- accept what the ghost says but do nothing;
- take on an "antic disposition";
- dismiss the ghost as an evil spirit and do nothing;
- kill himself ...

We can now consider the criteria for judging each of these. These might include:

- the effectiveness of the action;
- the practicability;
- the legality;
- the risk to himself;
- the risk to others;
- the cost;
- public opinion;
- utilitarian principles;
- deontological principles;
- libertarian principles.

Exploring the above can bring students of both subjects closer to the situation in which Hamlet finds himself. Taking the "kill Claudius" option, one way in which we could go through the criteria is as follows:

It's effective, in that it does what the ghost commands.

Practicability? This is very problematic, as Hamlet is not a killer, and Claudius is a king.

Legality? To kill a king! (Even if that king killed a king.)

Risk to himself? Potentially fatal.

Risk to others – could be great, particularly in the case of Gertrude, who might be implicated if the court takes Hamlet's side or, equally, if it doesn't. The cost? In most dilemmas in critical thinking we're talking about financial cost, but here there could be a huge cost to Hamlet's sense of who he is, if he takes the irrevocable step from the world of thinking to the world of murder; there could also be a huge cost to Gertrude and to Denmark itself, especially at a time of war.

What of public opinion? Claudius is the King; Claudius gives good parties; Claudius and Gertrude are two happy and united rulers.

Consider utilitarian principles: what about the quality of well-being resulting from any one of these choices? And for how many people?

Deontological principles? Perhaps this is the heart of the dilemma. Hamlet, according to the rules of his father's time, has a duty to his *father* to kill Claudius. Yet, as a man of the Renaissance rather than the Middle Ages, he has a duty to preserve, even celebrate life. On the other hand, is it his duty to the *state* to kill Claudius, because he is a murderer, or his duty to the state not to, because he is the King?

Finally, libertarian principles: the libertarian is concerned with liberty and the rights of the individual against the state, and this concerns Hamlet very much. He does all that he can to avoid being forced into becoming a killer, and yet berates himself for delaying his revenge.

Hamlet provides English and critical thinking students with an intimate contact with a thinker: thanks to the conventions of Elizabethan drama and the vehicle of the soliloquy, we have his arguments laid out clearly for us – including any faults.

In dealing with the "kill himself" option he appears to apply good thinking skills and yet, this "thinking too precisely" is not taking him any further towards a decision, merely postponing it:

Reasons "not to be":

- it's nobler to oppose and defeat pain;
- it would be like sleeping;
- the pain itself (does this contradict the first?): "the whips and scorns of time";
- "the oppressor's wrong";
- "the proud man's contumely";
- "the pangs of despised love";
- "the law's delay";
- "the insolence of office";
- "the spurns that patient merit of the unworthy takes ...";
- grunting and sweating under a weary life.

Reasons "to be":

- it's nobler to withstand the pain;
- if it's like sleeping it might involve uncontrolled dreaming (there's a useful exercise here on interrogating the analogy!);
- the dread of what comes next: "the undiscovered country";
- it's better to bear the ills we have rather than fly to unknown ones.

So – does this constitute an argument? Has he convinced himself of something? Where is its conclusion? It's in that line: " it is better to bear those ills we have than fly to others that we know not of".

What reasons support this conclusion?

There seem to be far more reasons for *not* being than being, but they're all neatly annulled by the conclusion; indeed even if he'd listed a hundred more, it would ironically only support the conclusion more, because all these things are knowable and known, and what happens after death isn't. So, it's not a bad piece of reasoning really.

In response to the dilemma about killing Claudius, how good a choice is suicide anyway? In terms of the effectiveness of the action it's a non-starter; if, however, Hamlet reconfigures the problem as "What's the best response to what the ghost told me?" it might be considered highly effective, as it removes him from an intolerable situation.

Practicability? Well, there seems to have been fairly easy access to poison in Elsinore, and no problem with weapons. Legality? Was suicide illegal in Elsinore? And would it matter if it were not?

The risk to himself? Well, mortal, but perhaps also the only thing that can save him from pain. But what about the risk of hell, especially likely for a suicide?

The risk to others? What effect would it have on his mother? Does this constitute a "risk"? It would certainly destroy her happiness – actually something he seems to want to achieve.

The cost – in this case not applicable. Public opinion – now, this is very important to Hamlet. What are his dying words? He won't let Horatio be the "antique Roman", because the story must be told. The truth must be revealed. If he killed himself, how could that happen?

Utilitarian principles? Even supposing it makes Hamlet happy – well, less desperately unhappy – it would benefit no-one else but perhaps Claudius, so that's not really compelling!

Duty? No, his duty is to stay alive and kill Claudius.

Liberty of the individual? Perhaps suicide is the ultimate expression of that. But Hamlet denies himself this freedom, takes on his "antic disposition" to give him time and later, when on his way to meet his death in England, shows a strong instinct for self-preservation. However, the carnage at the end of play provides a good illustration of what can happen when dilemmas are not resolved.

9
Words and Meaning

This chapter isn't about semiotics, linguistic analysis or A level English language. It gives a flavour of some of the activities and ideas from the (three-hour) session which English and critical thinking students participated in as part of an enrichment programme; there will be ideas here which English teachers (and critical thinking teachers) might like to try.

When the students arrived at the session they knew what its focus was to be. I handed out cards to small groups, each having a different quotation, phrase or idea on. The cards can simply be given out with no comment other than that the students should discuss what's on them in the light of the session's focus. The teacher can be more directive, though, and accompany each card with specific questions which the students address. (For example, *Women, Fire and Dangerous Things* refers to an aboriginal word which "means" all of them – and other things. What criteria link the three? What kind of category are they in?)

> "When I use a word," Humpty Dumpty said, in a rather scornful tone, "it means just what I choose it to mean – neither more nor less."

> A cheese sandwich is better than nothing.
> Nothing is better than eternal bliss.
> Therefore a cheese sandwich is better than eternal bliss.

Women, Fire and Dangerous Things –
by George Lakoff

Abortion is murder, so abortion is obviously wrong.

Christopher, in *The Curious Incident of the Dog in the Night-time* tells us he finds people confusing…
"This is for two main reasons.
The first main reason is that people do a lot of talking without using any words…
The second main reason is that people often talk using metaphors.
I laughed my socks off.
He was the apple of her eye.
They had a skeleton in the cupboard.
We had a real pig of a day.
The dog was stone dead.
The word metaphor means carrying something over from one place to another … and it is when you describe something by using a word for something that it isn't. This means that the word metaphor is a metaphor.
I think it should be called a lie because a pig is not like a day and people do not have skeletons in their cupboards. And when I try and make a picture of the phrase in my head it just confuses me because imagining an apple in someone's eye doesn't have anything to do with liking someone a lot and it makes you forget what the person was talking about."

ethnic cleansing

A person who has never had sight asks you to find a way of helping them to understand what "red", "blue", "green" or "yellow" are.

Understanding what words are doing is a key part of both the study of English and the study of critical thinking. Critical thinkers learn to spot equivocation – from the classic cheese sandwich example to more subtle and well-disguised attempts to win arguments by using a word in a different way in a different part of the argument or, to avoid using equivocation accidentally themselves, in their own arguments. English students, especially those studying literary texts, are reading a version of the language which is rich in metaphor, simile, allusion and ambiguity, although a critical thinking lesson (or three) can usefully look at metaphor, along with equivocation and vagueness.

There will, alas, always be plenty of examples of the inexact use of language for students to get their teeth into; students need to understand, though, that whereas vagueness can get in the way of clear thinking, the deliberate ambiguity of metaphor is about clarifying meaning. The difference is in intention and effect: vagueness, equivocation and lying can hide or distort the truth, whereas figurative language is most often used to reveal it and relies on precision. What sense would we make of the following, from Lawrence's *Women in Love*, if we didn't know what cymbals sounded like:

The locomotive, as if wanting to see what could be done, put on the brakes, and back came the trucks rebounding on the iron buffers, striking like horrible cymbals, clashing nearer and nearer in frightful strident concussions.

Or of this, from *Othello*, if we didn't understand what a pearl was?

...one whose hand,
Like the base Indian, threw a pearl away richer than all his tribe ...

In any subject, in any discussion or debate, it's very common to hear at some point someone saying "That's just semantics" – in other words, we're just arguing about what words mean. That's how most late night / early morning coffee-fuelled arguments tended to finish when I was an undergraduate. But semantics should never be preceded by "just" in this way, as if it's all rather a minor thing. Shouldn't we all have clear what we mean by something, in order that we can talk about it … meaningfully?

What does it mean, to mean? What's the meaning of meaning? Ask your students if they have ever looked it up in a dictionary. I've never had an affirmative answer to that; after all, it's a given that if we use a dictionary at all, we know what meaning means. Well, let's see … "signification; the thing intended; that which is in the mind or thoughts".

The meaning of any word, such as meaning, might, students assume, be determined or clarified by using a dictionary; but what we'll find there is more likely a collection of synonyms, and what we call reportive definitions. In critical thinking, however, and indeed in most academic studies, we might be more concerned with stipulative definitions, which establish or refine a definition for a particular purpose. An example of this would be, "For the purposes of this argument …" or "For the purposes of this policy, the policy holder is defined as …". We always begin our arguments in critical thinking by defining our terms.

Problems with communication can occur when reportive and stipulative definitions are mixed up. We may at college need very precise definitions of, say "student" in relation to funding, but in other contexts be perfectly happy with other definitions such as someone who is engaged in learning (surely, all of us?). What about "child"? When my parents and I go somewhere which charges an entry fee, say £5 for adults and £2 for children, could I not justifiably say that although I'm an adult (as defined legally) I'm also a child (as defined biologically – and emphasised by the presence of my parents)? Indeed, even were my parents not with me, I'm still their child.

Ask your students to consider that word "child" and see how many literal uses the word has. They might also consider figurative uses of the word; for example if we call a 55-year-old man a child we might be suggesting that he is *childish* – a derogatory term which would imply that some negative aspect of a child's behaviour were exhibited, or *childlike*, wherein a positive aspect, such as spontaneity, love of harmless fun or unselfconscious enjoyment of food were being referred to. Which did Kate Bush mean when she wrote about "The man with the child in his eyes"?

Other sorts of definitions are persuasive definitions, which imply a glossing over of terms, proceeding as if we all know what we mean and all agree. These often figure in fallacious arguments, often in arguments which beg the question, such as the "Abortion is murder" claim. This is a circular argument, relying on a highly persuasive and selective definition of "abortion".

Emotive language will add, or attempt to add, additional affective force, as opposed to reasoning. It doesn't necessarily weaken an argument, but can disguise weakness. "Stop cruelty to animals" is a sticker we might see on a back screen of a car; have you ever seen one saying the opposite? "Let's be cruel to animals, everybody. Join the league for cruel sports!" No, of course not. The whole debate rests on the *definition* of cruelty, which to some people would include keeping pets: even though they may live in luxury and be cuddled and cared for, they are in cages, out of their natural environment and, perhaps above all, away from their species.

If cruelty can be problematic to define, what about "health", "peace", "education", "freedom"? What about "love"? In the same session on language I put words such as these on cards and gave each one to a student to define; the others in the group challenged and helped to refine the definitions. Health, by the way, was there because of a difference of opinion I had with my husband. We were completing a survey about healthcare provision in our area and one of the questions asked if we had experienced any significant ill-health during the previous five years. I answered "no". "But you've just had back surgery!" "Yes, but I wasn't ill – that was just a mechanical problem." I didn't see having a disc taken out as curing ill-health; although I had been in excruciating pain and my life was made very difficult, I wasn't *ill*. My husband saw it as a malfunction which a healthy body wouldn't have. Discuss!

Another way with words is the euphemism, used to disguise or tone down negative connotations. Sometimes euphemisms are harmless, as when the person being addressed knows exactly what the euphemism is for (a bereaved person knows that someone referring to their partner's "passing" isn't trying to deny the truth, but merely trying to be gentle about it. Even saying you were deeply sorry to hear about someone's death is gentler than saying "I'm so sorry he's dead"). But in some cases euphemisms can, like emotive language, disguise and obfuscate. Is there anything more sickeningly euphemistic than "ethnic cleansing"? Cleansing is something I do with cleansing lotion. It's gentle and benign and necessary.

"Mining disaster" sounds like a natural occurrence (or, as some might say, an act of God) when it might have been caused by gross neglect on the part of an employer. So, euphemism can work both ways, as can semantic ambiguity. The latter is a key to metaphor and to jokes, but can also lead to bad argument, especially when the conclusion depends upon reasons which contain ambiguous words. Currently, Kate Moss is the face of Rimmel. One of the products which is advertised using her image is mascara. The inference we are to draw is that if we use Rimmel mascara we can be like Kate Moss. It is assumed that we want to be like her; we will therefore buy the mascara. Look at the word "like". If we buy the mascara and use it then there really *is* a way in which we are like Kate Moss (always assuming that she does actually use it). But that's the *only* way in which we'll be like her, isn't it? The only promise that can be kept is that if you use this mascara you'll be a Rimmel mascara user like Kate Moss. If Mike Tyson wore Rimmel mascara he too would be like Kate Moss, in that one respect.

10
Critical Thinking and Other Texts

We are English teachers. We want our students to read, anything. They will read if they enjoy it; we want them to enjoy reading. So we should give them enjoyable things to read, to help them develop an affinity for reading. Then we can make the reading a bit harder, which they may initially equate with less enjoyable, but by helping them to develop their reading skills we gradually make "harder" mean "at least as enjoyable" – and, maybe, "even more enjoyable". But we need to start at the right place. Whether it's a GCSE re-sit class or a new AS class, we can't assume that we have students who are comfortable with reading.

The film *Reservoir Dogs* provides a good introduction to AS critical thinking, starting as it does with an excellent and student friendly example of an argument. In using it for that subject it occurred to me that it would also work with new literature classes because although it sounds like natural dialogue it's scripted, naturalistic dialogue, well crafted in the same way as our literary texts are crafted. Showing the first few minutes of the film gives critical thinking students an argument to analyse; English students can use the same argument analysis to lead to an appreciation of the way Tarantino uses this part of the film to establish character – a key process for any dramatist. Show the first few minutes, but please let your students hear the music for the credits as well. It's part of their education.

The dialogue in the clip is very quick, so after we've watched it I give students a printed copy of the argument, from the screenplay, and we start our analysis. I ask, what's it about? What does Mr Pink want the others to accept, or agree with, or concede? What are Mr Pink's reasons? What are the counter arguments?

Mr Pink's conclusion is that it's acceptable for him not to tip. The others argue against this.

Mr Pink doesn't tip because:

1. He doesn't believe in it.
2. If the waitress isn't making enough money she can leave.
3. He tips when someone deserves a tip, not just because society says he should.
4. She didn't do anything special.
5. She only filled his cup three times.
6. The words "too busy" shouldn't be in a waitress's vocabulary.
7. They do make the minimum wage.
8. We don't tip at McDonald's, even though the staff there clean fryers.
9. Taxing tips may be wrong but it's nothing to do with him, or the issue.
10. They could get a better job if they trained – e.g. learning to type.

He should tip, say the others, because:

1. The wages are very low.
2. The girl was nice.
3. She might just have been too busy to fill Mr Pink's cup six times.
4. She's counting on tips to live.
5. The staff there work really hard.
6. They work harder than the people at McDonald's.
7. They're taxed on the tips they make.
8. Waitressing is the one job any woman can get and live on, because of the tips.

It's not Shakespeare. But it's a good argument. Critical thinkers will concentrate on the soundness of the two arguments; literature students can write a good paragraph on Mr Pink. They've also learnt something of the relationship between the characters, and a little about the others as individuals as well. It's deft and economical. It can introduce a short course on establishing character through dialogue, taking us as far as Shakespeare if we like.

Another film I recommend is *Thank You for Smoking*, written and directed by Jason Reitman, from the novel by Christopher Buckley. The film is described by Walter Chow, on his *filmfreak* site as being "for word junkies (English teachers?) and spin-doctors who get off on semantics and out-smarting debate opponents even when they're defending the weaker flank". And, "it's a beauty … about how easily we fall into moral ambiguity that exposes our moral ambiguity".

As I write I have been waiting five months for a copy of the screenplay, extracts from which I would have liked to have included here. But do look out for this funny, quirky outrageous film.

The leading character makes his living by being the voice of the tobacco industry of the United States. Why? Because it pays the mortgage ("the Yuppie Nurenberg defence") and because, above all else, he's so good at it. We really should despise him.

But he is clever, charming, witty and very skilful in subverting arguments to his own ends. We can interrogate his reasoning, while at the same time getting closer to his character and thereby to the characterisation – the skill of the writer in creating a fictional construct. This fictional construct is, apparently, one closely based on a real person. Jason Reitman recalls, on www.movienet.com, meeting the "real" Nick Naylor. Asked why Big Tobacco was thwarting a new law set to designate apartment buildings as either smoking or non-smoking he said, according to Reitman, "Well, this law is just another example of the rich trying to suppress the poor. Sure, if you're wealthy enough to afford a house, you can choose whether or not to smoke. But if you can't afford a house and are forced to rent, that choice … that right is taken away. Well, if there's anything we believe in … it's freedom. We will not stand by and watch as a person's rights are taken away."

When Nick goes to his son's school, invited along with other parents to tell them about what he does, one little girl tells him that her mother says cigarettes are really dangerous. He asks if the mother is a scientist. No. Is she a doctor? No. Ah, well she's not much of an expert, is she? Why should you do what she's telling you? In critical thinking terms, he's challenging her credibility – she has no relevant expertise – and suggesting that she is using an irrelevant appeal to authority. He turns to the class. How many of you like chocolate? Nearly all the hands go up. And if your mums and dads told you not to eat chocolate, would you stop? NO! Nick now shows us where this "argument" is heading: it's not about smoking, or about chocolate, but about making your own mind up and thinking for yourself. So he's not there as a self-confessed member of the "Merchants of Death" (representing the alcohol, firearms and tobacco lobbies) but as a champion of free thinking and personal choice. He's a true libertarian!

Nick's deft side stepping of valid arguments scintillate throughout the film. Watch out for the revelation that smoking actually saved his life!

Another very accessible text we can look at that shows us clever reasoning is *The Restaurant at the End of the Universe*, by the witty, wise, clever and much lamented Douglas Adams, whose *The Salmon of Doubt* is also a joy for critical thinkers – and any of us! The animal that wants to be eaten by Arthur Dent provides a lovely scenario for a debate. Arthur finds the whole idea repugnant, but he's defeated by the logic of it. Earlier in the book Zaphod Beebelbrox, so cool an intergalactic being that he needs two heads in order to wear two pairs of shades, is in a spot of bother, which he leaves Marvin, the depressed robot, to deal with. Marvin is hopelessly inadequate to the task in terms of his physical resources; all he has to defeat the Frogstar Scout robot class D is his brain which, fortunately, is "the size of a planet".

> 'Out of my way, little robot,' growled the tank.
> 'I'm afraid,' said Marvin, 'that I've been left here to stop you.'
> … 'What are you armed with?' roared the tank in disbelief.
> 'Guess,' said Marvin.
> (Ask, why is this such a smart move? What understanding does it show on the part of Marvin? Remember that Marvin has been (reluctantly) in the company of non-robots for a long time.)
> 'Guess?' said the tank.
> 'Yes, go on,' said Marvin to the huge battle machine, 'you'll never guess.'
> (Is this an appeal to ignorance? What you can't know must be really bad!)

'Errmmm …' said the machine, vibrating with unaccustomed thought,
(there's a clue!) *'laser beams?'*
Marvin shook his head solemnly.
(This is because it's true, but Marvin's aura of confidence is trying to imply that whatever the robot comes up with, Marvin has something much better.)
'No,' muttered the machine in its deep guttural rumble, 'Too obvious. Anti-matter ray?' it hazarded.
(Marvin has the machine uncertain, and also he is gaining crucial time for Zaphod.)
'Far too obvious,' admonished Marvin.
(He hasn't had to admit that he doesn't actually have an anti-matter ray, of course; the inference drawn by the robot is that he has.)

The robot continues to try and guess what it is that Marvin has, until Marvin appears to become indulgent:

'You're thinking along the wrong lines,' said Marvin, 'You're failing to take into account something fairly basic in the relationship between men and robots.'
(The Frogstar tank doesn't get this.)
'Just think,' urged Marvin, 'they left me, an ordinary, menial robot, to stop you, a gigantic heavy-duty battle machine, whilst they ran off to save themselves. What do you think they would leave me with?'
'Oooh er,' muttered the machine in alarm, 'something pretty damn devastating I should expect.'
'Expect!' said Marvin, 'Oh yes, expect. I'll tell you what they gave me to protect myself with shall I?'
'Yes, alright,' said the battle machine, bracing itself.
(Which shows how successful Marvin's strategy has been thus far.)
'Nothing,' said Marvin.
There was a dangerous pause.
(Within which, ask your students what Marvin's up to now.)
'Nothing?' roared the battle machine.
'Nothing at all,' intoned Marvin dismally, 'not an electronic sausage.'
The machine heaved about with fury.
'Well, doesn't that just take the biscuit!' it roared, 'Nothing, eh? Just don't think, do they?'

'And me,' said Marvin in a low soft voice, 'with this terrible pain in all the diodes down my left side.'

'Makes you spit, doesn't it?'

'Yes,' agreed Marvin, with feeling.

'Hell, that makes me angry,' bellowed the machine, 'think I'll smash that wall down!'

The electron ram stabbed out another searing blaze of light and took out the wall next to the machine.

'How do you think I feel?' said Marvin bitterly.

'Just ran off and left you, did they?' the machine thundered.

'Yes,' said Marvin.

'I think I'll shoot down their bloody ceiling as well!' raged the tank.

It took out the ceiling of the bridge.

'That's very impressive,' murmured Marvin.

'You ain't seen nothing yet,' promised the machine, 'I can take out this floor too, no trouble!'

It took out the floor too.

'Hell's bells!' the machine roared as it plummeted fifteen storeys and smashed itself to bits on the ground below.

'What a depressingly stupid machine,' said Marvin, and trudged away.

Invite students to evaluate his strategy in dealing with this "depressingly stupid machine". Look at Adams' writing – like Tarantino's it is deft and economical. He creates a brief relationship between Marvin and the tank, and Marvin tricks it into using its weaponry for its own destruction. This is clever stuff on Marvin's part!

What can we do with this as a piece of text, in our introduction to AS literature? Characters using reasoning set against characters who don't? Writers using moments of danger or crisis to highlight a particular characteristic? At this point of grave danger, we see Marvin at his best: what about other texts in which a writer puts his or her characters under pressure, allowing us to see their heightened responses? Soap writers do this all the time, but Shakespeare's not bad at it either. Antic disposition comes to mind, for example, then there's murdering sleep; howl howl howl; the odd suicide. Students could begin to compile a file of extracts in which characters are put to the test. These will be dramatic moments which call on writers' skills to recreate emotional intensity or flashes of insight. This could include poetry, of course, as an intensifier by virtue of its conflation of much into little.

So, here's a possible introduction to reading, using *Reservoir Dogs*, *Thank You for Smoking*, *The Restaurant at the End of the Universe*, and extracts from half a dozen Shakespeare plays!

11

Introducing Critical Thinking to an English Literature Class

There are two ways of introducing approaches and skills from critical thinking to students of literature. One is to wait until a point arises where it is natural to introduce the idea. For example, on reading a poem, and trying various ways into it, the idea of the poem as an argument could be put forward. It would be at this point that the use of the word "argument" in critical thinking could be explained, with some illustrations to help clarify the structure and elements. Thus the poem comes first and the approach arises from it. The same can happen with applying credibility criteria to a claim, claimant or evidence, as in the approaches outlined elsewhere to *Othello*, *Much Ado About Nothing* and *Measure for Measure*. The alternative is to start with the critical thinking, establishing a few key points and then moving on to the texts as illustrations of those points, and as texts to which the critical thinking analysis can be applied. Initially I used the former approach, simply because my own engagement with critical thinking and my ideas about bringing its skills to literature study were emerging, developing more with each text and each class's experience. However, I have subsequently experimented with the latter approach, with interesting results.

The first time I did this was with a class normally taught by a colleague. This was simply because I wanted to work with AS students at this point and didn't have any of my own.

The class had been studying *High Windows*, and all they knew was that they were going to be looking at a different way of reading Larkin. What did I hope they would learn? The overall aim was to introduce them to a different way of reading; to do this I planned to look at basic argument structure (i.e. claims and inferences, or reasons and conclusions), arguments with unstated reasons, (assumptions) and perhaps the hypothetical reasoning of conditional syllogisms (If … then …). I planned to use some of the poems which are explored in detail in the earlier chapter on poetry, and I planned to include an opportunity for the students to experiment with this new approach. I had an hour and a quarter, and I got about a quarter of all that done: this was more like a week's lessons really!

The first thing I did was ask, "Has anyone had an argument today?" It was 11 o'clock, and I was surprised when no hands went up. "How about in the last few days?" Plenty more this time! The next question was, "Has anyone *constructed* an argument over the last few days?" No hands. Immediately we have something interesting to follow up. The third question, "Has anyone *analysed* one?" drew the same response. What we were establishing here was their understanding of the word argument. It evidently included neither writing essays nor deconstructing texts.

I had the verbs "have" "construct" and "analyse" on the board, leaving them there without comment for the time being.

The next question was, "Does anyone here do maths?" Most of them laughed at that question; one student put his hand up. I asked the others what they saw as some of the differences between maths and literature, in both content and method of learning. I then asked the maths student to add his thoughts. The responses were very interesting for what they revealed about the students' perceptions of mathematics. Suggestions included, "Maths means the same everywhere, but literature can be interpreted differently" and "In maths you're trying to get the right answer, but in literature you're trying to come to your own interpretation." I was only to be with the class for one lesson, and so on this occasion resisted the temptation to open up discussion on these points. However, it's something I have subsequently pursued and hope to write about in the future.

Next, on the board, I wrote:

All As are B.
C is not B.
Therefore ?

The answer, "C is not A!" came out … from the maths student.

To emphasise that we were looking at structure at this stage, rather than content, I added something that was clearly not true:

All Venusians are blue.
Zog is green (i.e. not blue)
Therefore?

And there were lots of calls of "Zog isn't a Venusian". (Come to an English lesson and learn that a non-existent being can't be from Venus.) (Sounds like fiction to me!)

Another one:

If A then B.
Not A.
Therefore?

"Not B?" with a rising tone rather than an exclamation mark.

I turned to my colleague, who would normally have been teaching the class:

> "If Jamie is teaching this class then he is happy.
> He isn't teaching this class.
> So …?"

Pause for thought while they discussed whether it would be, "So, he isn't happy". They asked him, are you happy? He said yes, he was very happy, even though he wasn't teaching them. And then the response came back, "Well, you can't say therefore Jamie's not happy. Just because he's happy when he teaches us it doesn't mean that other things can't make him happy." Ah! So the structure is wrong. (I didn't introduce the phrase "denying the antecedent": too much, too soon.)

What, I suggested you may be wondering, has any of this to do with *High Windows*?

"Well, poems have structures, they're organised in a certain way."
Something's happening here!

At this point I asked the students to think back to the argument that they had
had most recently. I gave them a straightforward definition of argument, as a
conclusion which is supported by one or more reasons, the conclusion being
drawn from or inferred from the reasons. I explained that if we accepted the
reasons, and the conclusion was drawn from those reasons, we would have to
accept the conclusion. Here was one such argument provided by a student:

Mother: You're not going to college in that top!
Daughter: Why not?
Mother: It's freezing cold and there's nothing to it.
Daughter: But –
Mother: Go and get something else on, NOW!

What's the mother's "conclusion" … what does she want her daughter to
accept, be persuaded to do? Change her top.

You must change your top because …? What reason did she give to support
her conclusion? That it's cold and that the top is skimpy. Was it cold? Yes.
Was it skimpy? Yes. So, why did you try to argue for a different conclusion
(i.e. that you should be allowed to wear the top)? What reasons might you
have given? You couldn't challenge her reasons; you've just agreed that they
were true. And if you accept the reasons, surely you must accept the
conclusion? How might you have constructed a counter argument which
would have used reasoning to change her mind?

Here is an opportunity to introduce assumptions. "What must your mum have
been assuming, have taken to be the case, that she hasn't stated?" Responses
included, "That I wasn't going to wear a coat" and, "That it's not very warm
in college." OK, what happens if we make those unstated reasons into stated
ones? We get:

R1:   It is very cold.
R2:   That top is very skimpy.
R3:   You won't wear a coat.
R4:   College isn't very warm.

C: Therefore you should not wear that top.

Now, is it a bit easier to see how you could have countered her argument? "Yes, by putting her straight about the coat and the temperature in college." Then would she have been persuaded, through your reasoning? "NO CHANCE!" came the reply, "She'd have still got her way." Here's a nice opportunity to mention our first fallacy: an appeal to authority.

Critical thinking helps us to understand the difference between good reasoning and faulty reasoning. Spotting other people's flaws and fallacies is part of this. I asked, "Has anyone ever heard these words, 'You would say that, you're a girl', or 'What do you know, you're only 17?' ... attacking the arguer, not the argument. Next time that happens smile secretly to yourself and think, 'Well, you've lost this one if the best you can do is to attack me instead of my argument.'"

Ad hominem, literally, to the man, went on the board, followed by *straw man*, *over generalisation, tu quoque* and *slippery slope*. I gave examples of each of those; all were recognised by the students. Then I added equivocation, using the cheese sandwich and eternal happiness example. (A cheese sandwich is better than nothing. Nothing is better than [students can make their own suggestions here]. Therefore a cheese sandwich is better than [winning the lottery, Hull City being promoted, Christmas, a life of health and happiness ...].) Students then had the opportunity to recall any examples of these which they'd heard, read or, perhaps, used themselves.

One student observed that equivocation and metaphor were a bit similar, and we spent the next ten minutes taking this further. Again, it could have been a whole lesson, in other circumstances; it is indeed part of a whole separate chapter in this book.

By this point we've discovered that critical thinking is to do with reasoning. That reasoning has a structure as well as content. We have a definition of argument. We've learnt a new meaning of assumption. We've learnt about some ways in which reasoning can be flawed ... but what's all this got to do with literature?

I asked a few of the students to read out the annotations they'd made around the poem 'This Be the Verse'. There were comments about tone, the poet's attitude, demotic language, taboo language, phonology, simile and verse form. It was, quite properly, all about what the poet was saying and how he was saying it. The "how" was explored within a linguistic framework comprising phonology, lexis, semantics, grammar, syntax and pragmatics. But my question was, "What's he wanting us to accept, or do?"; "What is he hoping to persuade us of?"

And then we worked through the poem as illustrated in detail in Chapter 7.

Implicit in the question, "How much critical thinking do your students need to know?" is "and you as well?" This isn't a comprehensive book on critical thinking, on what it is and how it can be taught. There are other works which will help with that, which are listed elsewhere. If you are an English teacher working with my book you have, I hope, enough explanations and examples of critical thinking terms, structures and applications to enable you to introduce them to your students. You might even discover that there are critical thinking students in your English classes, and be able to involve them in lessons. Do they make any connections between the two subjects? Here's an account of one example of a student bringing a "critical thinking" approach to a task set in literature.

The Sublime Mystery…

OK then you lot! At the beginning of term I was set a task. The task was to find out exactly what "the sublime" is. As you will see from your packs, I have pieced together various bits of evidence in my search to discover what "the sublime" is. I have drawn my findings into a conclusion, which I would not like you to look at until the end! Because I am still not fully sure myself what this mysterious sublime is, I would like you guys to assess my evidence and to come up with your own conclusion as to what the sublime is. When you have finished doing this we can compare our conclusions and see if they are similar. Only then will we truly have solved the mystery of the sublime!

Second year students were studying *Lyrical Ballads*. It was the focus for a part of the syllabus which looks at the relationship between text and context, and each student had chosen, from a list which I gave them, a particular contextual aspect to explore. They were then to devise a way of presenting what they had found. Some chose to look at Burns, or Blake, others chose the American War of Independence or the French Revolution; one chose Kant, another Gothic, another Rousseau; some the art of the period, others the music; some the Enlightenment, others poetic form. Bethany, not a critical thinking student but a student who had been taught by me, an English teacher using critical thinking as part of her teaching, chose "the sublime". She chose this because she didn't think she knew anything about it, whereas many of the others had made their choices for precisely the opposite reason. Each motive gave rise to some excellent work; I want to describe Beth's in particular because it illustrates a way in which critical thinking can enhance work in literature.

Beth had read and researched, and had worked hard to come to a definition of the sublime which was based on "evidence", that is the thoughts and ideas of others, as illustrated in the poems. She arrived at the lesson with brown envelopes, filled with lots of bits of paper, including the one the text of which is reproduced above.

In groups the students read her instruction, took out all the bits of paper with the ideas, quotations and questions on, and began piecing them together in their own way. Beth wasn't telling them what the sublime was, or what it meant, nor its significance in relation to *Lyrical Ballads*; she wasn't even telling them at this stage what she *thought* it meant. The groups discussed the statements, the "claims" we might say, and the "evidence" from the poems. They did various things with them, such as interrogating them, deciding whether the claims were supported by the poems, and ordering them using a hierarchy of significance. They looked for consistency and inconsistency of definition or explanation. The discussion went on for a very productive and lively half hour, and then each group reported to the class what they had discovered and what conclusion they had drawn. "Discovered" and "drawn" are key to this: they were active in coming to their understanding, rather than passively absorbing what someone else had told them. Beth didn't tell them what the sublime was; she gave them the opportunity to find out for themselves. At the end of the process she gave them her "conclusion": and no, I'm not telling you – you'll have to work it out for yourself!

I wonder what Ofsted would have given Bethany as a grade for this lesson?

The bits of paper being placed and replaced all over the tables recalls a revision lesson on *Enduring Love*. I took the brief chapter summaries of one or two sentences each which can be found on the excellent www.teachit.co.uk website and cut them up, so that each chapter was on a separate strip of paper. I gave a set of the strips to each group of students within the class, and their challenge was to put them in the right order – that is, the order in which they appear in the book. They were up on their feet, round the tables, discussing, disputing and recalling. The exercise is a simple one in revising the book's plot and narrative structure; it also helps students to understand how well (or otherwise) they know this. This was especially important as the examination would be taken without the book being available.

The benefits of the exercise were enhanced when one or two chapters were placed in the wrong order, as this lead to discussion about how that might alter our understanding of the text, and how a different narrative structure influences the way we make meaning and the meaning that we make.

This is very like an exercise which seems to work well in the early stages of critical thinking, in which each part of an argument is written separately, on card and in letters large enough to be read across a classroom. If the argument has, say, eight parts (conclusion, intermediate conclusion, counter argument, three reasons, one piece of evidence and a principle), ask for eight volunteers. The chances are that you have the same people volunteering for things every time you ask; this is a neat way of turning the tables on the others. The volunteers have a card each (it's a good idea to have a conclusion which doesn't begin "Therefore") and they stand in a line, holding up the cards for the rest to see. The parts of the argument are not, of course, in the right order. Now, it's the *rest* of the class who have to do the thinking – to direct the others to move along the line in order to create the best sequence. It's a fun way of looking at argument structure, with the potential for lots of movement. It gives a very clear idea of how moving one component can affect the others: "No, if he moves there then she's in the wrong place … go back to where you were before …".

This can then be tried with the students' own writing (whether in critical thinking or English), to help them think about the significance of an effective structure in which there is a clear sense of order and development. It can enable them to think about how different structuring of the same points can create different emphases. They can do this with their own work, but it also works collaboratively, where the separate points are given to someone else to read and order, and where the writer and "editor" then confer to share their thoughts. Just like in the case of Bethany's lesson, the students are not being told but are discovering. And there's surely a touch of the sublime about that.

12

Using Critical Thinking Approaches to (post-16) GCSE English

Should cannabis be legalised?

Yes, because:

- it clears your lungs;
- there would be less drugs related crime;
- it's better than five fruit and vegetables a day;
- it's a great pain relief;
- it would be easier to buy;
- people wouldn't be bothering with big drugs;
- it's a growing plant that God created. If He didn't want anyone to smoke it He wouldn't have put it there;
- It's better than alcohol.

No, because:

- you would have to pay tax on it;
- younger people may take a liking to it;
- it damages brain cells;
- it causes skitsefrenia;
- Tony Blair and the Queen would be pot heads.

I've tidied up the spelling and grammar (apart from the perfect phonetic spelling of schizophrenia), otherwise this is exactly what a student in a GCSE re-sit class produced in preparation for a class debate. Apart from the insight it gives into the perception of a 17-year-old girl, and the value it has had in providing argument analysis for A level critical thinking, it is an example of why critical thinking skills are important, and should be introduced and practised at all levels.

All English teachers working with GCSE students, whether post-16 in my case or in Years 10 or 11, will encourage class discussion and will probably use debates as a means of both improving and assessing students' speaking and listening skills. Written papers invite students to "argue or persuade" and it's important to help them understand what those two words mean and what the distinctions and relationships are between the skills.

It wasn't until I started teaching critical thinking that I began to teach reasoning skills to the re-sit class as a discrete topic, beginning with the "robbery" exercise.

When students start their re-sit course they may well be feeling a bit low. After all, re-sits are not elective and the students thought they were coming to college to *choose* what they would do. They may feel that they have failed and they may be quite hurt and defensive; they may be desperate to do well, but not know what they can do better than they did at school. It's important, therefore, to establish a sense of the course being fresh and to establish a sense of trust, in which the classroom is seen as being a safe place for collaborative learning, a safe place for stepping out of the comfort zone of failure.

I first came across the "robbery" exercise through Roy van den Brink-Budgen, but neither he nor I know its origin. Typing it into the very useful www.texthunter.co.uk site revealed how ubiquitous it is, but not its provenance. If the person who wrote it is reading this, or is known to anyone reading this, I'd be grateful to hear, so that I can acknowledge the authorship. The version below has 15 statements; other versions have one or two more. If you haven't seen it before, try it yourself before reading what follows it!

A businessman had just turned off the lights in the store when a man appeared and demanded money. The owner opened a cash register. The contents of the cash register were scooped up and the man sped away. A member of the police force was notified promptly.

Decide whether the statements below are true, false or can't be known. Write T, F and ? as appropriate.

1. A man appeared after the owner had turned off the store lights.
2. The robber was a man.
3. The man who appeared did not demand money.
4. The man who opened the cash register was the owner.
5. The store owner scooped up the contents of the cash register and ran away.
6. Someone opened a cash register.
7. After the man who had demanded the money scooped up the contents of the cash register, he ran away.
8. While the cash register contained money, the story does not state how much.
9. The robber demanded money of the owner.
10. The robber opened the cash register.
11. After the store lights were turned off a man appeared.
12. The robber did not take the money with him.
13. The robber did not demand money of the owner.
14. The owner opened the cash register.
15. The story contains a series of events in which only three people are referred to: the owner of the store, a man who demanded money and a member of the police force.

Hand out the "robbery" exercise. Tell the students that it has to be done in silence and that on no account may they look at anyone else's work as they are doing it. (This is an introduction to a course which will draw heavily on collaboration, peer learning and peer assessment: just stay with me!) After they have done the exercise the students need to add up the numbers of "true" and "false" and the number of question marks. They then need to come out and record the totals against their names. This can either be done on a board or on a computer linked to a screen. What's important is that everyone can see everyone's results. (If this is the first lesson it's also a helpful way to start learning names.) It's useful to see who finished quickly, and later to see if there is any correlation between speed and accuracy.

Making public the answers is potentially disconcerting: everyone will know if they're wrong! But surely a teacher wouldn't do that to them? To humiliate them in front of the others? There must be another reason for doing it this way.

The reason begins to emerge when the first brave one comes out to the front. I would look at the totals and respond with, "That's interesting. While you're waiting for the others just have another look." "Interesting" is probably annoyingly enigmatic: we want to know if it's right or wrong!

Experience suggests that as soon as the next person comes out we'll have a different set of totals. This enables the teacher to say something like, "Right – two very different scores. Both of you have a think about how this could be – after all, it's only a four line story."

As they eventually finish, we have a look at the results. Scores from recent classes have ranged from one extreme – no question marks – to nine.

Usually there are very few question marks. Does our education system encourage students in the belief that "I don't know" is a bad answer? One of the benefits to accrue from this exercise is that we can begin to disabuse them of that. In learning we must start with what the students know, and build on it; at the same time we must help them to understand that knowing what we don't know is also an important component of learning.

The next thing to do is to pick out the most extreme answers: now, Sam's only got one question mark and Tim's got six. There are six things that Tim says he doesn't know or can't know, but which Sam is sure of. Tim, which are the six with question marks? Sam, out of those, pick one which you've given a definite "true" or "false" to. We'll then hear Sam's answer and ask Tim to explain why he's put a question mark … What did anyone else get for that one? After some discussion, minds are beginning to change. Ask them to do the exercise again, and as before to come out and record their answers. **Invariably** the number of question marks increases.

The next move might be to ask students to share their papers with the person next to them, and see if they can come to any agreement about any that they have different answers to.

Finally, we go through the questions together, and reach the conclusion that we can only be sure of four things.

1. We don't know that the owner turned off the store lights: we can't assume that the businessman and the owner are one and the same.
2. We don't know that a robbery has even taken place (perhaps the man was owed the money?).
3. This we know to be false.
4. We don't know that the owner is a man.
5. Use of the passive voice means we don't know who did the scooping. (Perhaps the man demanding money; perhaps the owner, trying to save it from being taken.)
6. This we know to be true.
7. We can't know this – see 5.
8. We don't know what was in the cash register. Probably money, but it could have been vouchers, for example.
9. We can't know this – see 2.
10. As above.
11. This we know to be true.
12. See 2 and 5 and 8.
13. See 2. Also, we aren't told to whom the demand was addressed.
14. This we know to be true.
15. See 1.

Thus we have one false statement, three true, and eleven about which we can't know.

What's been going on here? Firstly, we've learnt that it's OK to say "I don't know." Secondly, that we can learn from each other. Thirdly, we've learnt that it's worth looking again and thinking again. Fourthly, we've risen to a challenge, solved a conundrum. Finally, we've begun to see that we need to read carefully, and we are on the edge of learning about assumptions, which come next.

In critical thinking we use the word "assumption" specifically to mean a reason which isn't stated in an argument, but which the "author" of the argument must believe in order to come to his or her conclusion. In the previous chapter I described introducing critical thinking to literature students and I gave an example of an argument between a mother and daughter about what is appropriate to wear for college. The same thing can be done with the GCSE students, or we can use the "polar bear" argument, which is as ubiquitous as the "robbery" exercise. Other large and dangerous animals may be substituted. I used a tiger last time, as Hull City AFC are known as the Tigers (the relevance of this will become apparent!).

We use the robbery exercise to introduce assumption. What sort of things did you assume to be true, in order to come to your judgements? I tell them what I mean by an assumption, and we talk about how *useful* they can be, and how much time they can save, but how we must be very sure that they are correct assumptions before we act on them.

Shout out to one of the students, "Watch out! There's a tiger behind you!" Ask, "What's the thing I want you to do?" "Watch out." "We'll call that a conclusion to an argument. Am I giving you a reason why you should watch out?" "Yes, there's a tiger behind me."

But then we need to think about whether that's enough. Is it a convincing argument? Is there anything I could be assuming that would actually make it a bad argument? Are there any assumptions which would make my conclusion silly? Some suggestions which students have made are listed below.

It could be:

- a stuffed tiger (although perhaps even a stuffed tiger would hurt you if it fell on your head);
- a toy tiger;
- your pet tiger;
- a Hull City player.

So I must be assuming that it isn't any one of those.

I'm also assuming:

- that you can hear;

- that you understand what I'm saying;

- that you aren't suicidal, and haven't waited for hours to tempt this tiger to come up behind you and maul you to death.

Now we look back at the passage and at all the things we've assumed, starting with the idea that the scenario is about a robbery!

This is a really nice lesson to start with; it sets the tone I want to establish and endure through the course. It changes our direction – we're going to do English through things that are clear, using skills that can be learnt.

It may be that students have got disappointing results because they just don't know what it is that they're doing when they do English. I've often heard them say that you can't really revise for a GCSE English exam, and in a way they are right – there isn't a lot of content to learn and re-visit. But what they can do is to learn skills and practise them: skills of good inferential reading, of organising thoughts and writing in an ordered, logical way, of discussing and arguing soundly. There's still plenty of room for being imaginative and creative, and for being tentative in some aspects of the course, but knowing that they can learn the skills of reasoning will give them security. Working with groups on the poetry anthology, for example, reveals that some (more often female students) are comfortable with skills like interpreting, can handle poems having multiple possibilities and respond to the deliberate ambiguity of metaphor; others (more often male) enjoy looking at the poems as argument, rather as we can with the A level texts.

And now, back to cannabis! This argument was actually the result of quite a lot of work on the part of the student, whom I'll call Rachel. The class had chosen the topic for debate and it was obvious why some of them were very interested in it. They had a vested interest in cannabis being legalised. At first there was a free-for-all, with claims, counter claims and unsupported assertions flying round the room; apocryphal stories and anecdotes flowed freely. Seeking to establish order out of chaos, we agreed a few rules of argument. We did work on writing an argument that was both deductively valid and sound, or at least inductively forceful and sound. We talked about using evidence to support reasons and about how we might judge whether that evidence was credible and relevant. We looked at counter arguments. Rachel's first attempt at writing her argument at least has some clarity, and if we accepted her reasons we would have to accept her conclusion. But did we accept her reasons? What would she need to do to make us accept them? Clearly, she had to go and find evidence to support the point about the lungs, the five-a-day and alcohol (and define "better" as well); the group accepted the point about pain relief on the basis of having heard evidence from MS sufferers referred to in the media. We noted the hypothetical reasoning she had used: if we legalised cannabis then there would be less drug-related crime, and looked at the current situation where cannabis is not legal and there is a lot of drug-related crime. But we needed to delve into the soundness of that reasoning. Can we say that one is the cause of the other, and that therefore a change affecting one would mean a change in the other? They felt that this was a reasonable thing to do, but only if the legal cannabis were cheaper than the currently illegal cannabis: we accepted that it would be easier to buy – but acknowledged that being easier to buy wouldn't mean that it was easier to afford. Another piece of hypothetical reasoning suggested that if cannabis were legal people wouldn't get involved in hard drugs. We would need to look at ways of supporting this claim. The point about it being a growing plant was interesting. Is the fact that something exists a reason for regarding it as a good thing? We had quite a philosophical discussion on that one! We thought we'd have to leave God out of it, as we couldn't use reasoning on matters of faith, by definition.

The counter argument was going very well until the last reason, but then again, it made us laugh.

Rachel was a good sport in letting us go through her argument like this, (and letting me use it in this chapter) and she went away to search for evidence and bring her argument back. Sadly, she and the college parted company shortly after, but the class carried on the work for her and sought to find evidence to support the claims about five a day, alcohol and clearing the lungs. We also had some fun with a creative writing piece based on the final reason in the counter argument!

There are some schools and colleges which only offer A level critical thinking to the students with the highest prior achievement. They get high grades in the AS, which is positive for them and helpful to their institution's standing. But *all* students need to have access to the tools of reasoning. All students need to be able to spot fallacious arguments, if they are not to be taken advantage of by those who are setting out to deceive them. However, that doesn't mean that the cynical approach adopted by other institutions should be applauded: that as critical thinking is largely content free, it can be taught to anybody, by anybody, with consequent funding advantages. Well, it *can* be taught by anybody, to anybody – badly.

To take such a valuable skill, something which can truly enable young people to have more control over what happens to them, and either deny it to them because they are not an elite group or to put them in a situation where they could find themselves being "taught" by someone who has no interest in, let alone understanding of the subject, is a cynical insult to them and is the opposite of education. We should help all students to think better and reason better; should be prepared to invest time and money in introducing teachers to ways in which they can help students think critically. We shouldn't pressgang teachers to teach it just because they have "spare" hours, and then give them no training or support or resources. If all else fails, we should look at ways in which the skills of critical thinking can be developed through other subjects. Mmm – I think I'm writing a book about this!

Appendix

RECOMMENDED READING

Bennett, Deborah (2005). *Logic Made Easy*. London: Penguin Books Ltd. This does just what it says on the tin.

Brink-Budgen, Roy van den
  (2000). *Critical Thinking for Students*. Oxford: How To Books.
  (2005). *Critical Thinking for AS Level*. Oxford: How To Books.
  (2006). *Critical Thinking for A2*. Oxford: How To Books.
These three are core texts for the A level and are now complemented by a DVD and a complete on-line course: www.criticalthinkingonline.co.uk

Stewart, Noel *Ethics: an introduction* Cambridge: Polity (pub. autumn 2008).
Written for A level and undergraduate philosophy students but very accessible; the only book on ethics which has made me laugh out loud (see, for example, the conversation between Fabio Capello and Socrates on "victory" and the England manager's subsequent talk to his bewildered team).

Thomson, Anne (1999). *Critical Reasoning in Ethics: a practical introduction*. Abingdon: Routledge.

Warburton, Nigel (1996). *Thinking from A to Z*. Abingdon: Routledge. A very clear alphabetical reference for critical thinking terms.

Index

Index of texts